A NEW VOICE OF YOUTH

THE ONE

DAVID ASSCHERICK AND TY GIBSON

An Evangelistic Youth Series Resource

TWELVE PRESENTATIONS

Complete With Small Group Discussion Starters

Jesus. Explore some of the most
illuminating and incandescent truths about
His person, character, and ministry.

REVIEW AND HERALD® PUBLISHING ASSOCIATION

Since 1861 | www.reviewandherald.com

Resources

with

Small Group Discussions

for

Youth Evangelistic Series

Printed by Review and Herald® Publishing Association, Hagerstown, MD 21741-1119

Sermons by David Asscherick and Ty Gibson
Discussion guides by Debbonnaire Kovacs
Project directed by Gilbert Cangy
Copyedited by Erica Jones
Cover design by Daniel Anez / Review and Herald® Design Center
Interior design by Maria Dunchie

PRINTED IN U.S.A.

18 17 16 15 14   5 4 3 2 1

Library of Congress Control Number: 2014932789

ISBN 978-0-8280-2794-6

To order, **call** 1-800-765-6955.

Visit us at **www.reviewandherald.com** for information on other Review and Herald® products.

THE CONCEPT

behind The One is that Jesus Christ

is revealed in Scripture

as multidimensional in His various saving roles.

He is Creator.

And King.

And Savior.

And Healer.

And more.

He is The One,

but like a multihued and multifaceted diamond,

He is beautiful,

and yet,

a little different from every angle.

Table of Contents

The Foreword......................9

Why This Book?......................11

Hints from Ty and Dave......................13

1. THE MAKER......................14

    The Point: Examining creation, trinity, and the character of God
    Scripture Base: Genesis 1:1

2. THE COMMUNICATOR......................28

    The Point: The Bible is God's Word of love and self-revelation
    Scripture Base: John 15:15

3. THE KING......................40

    The Point: The law and government of God
    Scripture Base: Luke 12:37

4. THE SAVIOR......................54

    The Point: The fall, the nature of sin, and the gift of salvation
    Scripture Base: Genesis 3:15

5. THE SPIRIT......................70

    The Point: The role of the Holy Spirit
    Scripture Base: John 14:15-18

6. **THE GREAT GIVER**....................**86**

   The Point: The gift and blessings of the Sabbath

   Scripture Base: Genesis 2:1-3

7. **THE HEALER**....................**104**

   The Point: Healthful living

   Scripture Base: John 10:10

8. **THE SACRIFICE**....................**118**

   The Point: Death, hell, and the cross

   Scripture Base: 2 Corinthians 5:21

9. **THE NEW MAN**..............................**136**

   The Point: A new life in Christ

   Scripture Base: Galatians 2:20

10. **THE MESSAGE**....................**148**

   The Point: The three angels' messages

   Scripture Base: Revelation 14:6, 7

11. **THE BRIDEGROOM**....................**164**

   The Point: Jesus' second coming

   Scripture Base: Revelation 14:1-3

12. **THE BODY**....................**178**

   The Point: Church, discipleship, and the great commission

   Scripture Base: 1 Corinthians 12:27

Foreword

It has been a while since we last produced an evangelistic series for young people. The *Voice of Youth*, which used to be an essential part of the senior youth ministry , is now just a distant memory for many, while in more recent times, the Elijah project caught the imagination of youth groups globally.

The recent outreach trends in youth ministry have gravitated towards a more practical model, as evidenced by initiatives such as Impact, Storm Co, Compassion Movement, Global Youth Day and the likes. Drawing from Ellen White's reference that "Christ's method alone will bring true success in reaching people," a stronger emphasis has been placed on the Good Samaritan perspective in reaching out to be the hands and feet of Jesus.

While this fresh and valid approach is most welcomed, personal verbal witness and the public proclamation of the Word of God is still at the heart of our evangelistic adventures. Jesus both demonstrated and proclaimed the kingdom of God. It is time for something new, fresh, relevant and provocative to arrest the attention of our world in desperate need of hope.

David Asscherick and Ty Gibson have combined their creativity, experience, and passion for Jesus in the production of *The One*. This riveting evangelistic series places the spotlight on the central character of the Scriptures, the Lord Jesus Himself. It explores the beauty of grace and examines the multidimensional roles that He assumed in stooping down to save us and lifting our sight to the glory that is to come because of Him.

I trust that by the grace of God and the power of His Spirit, *The One* will bring new and fresh interest and impetus to the proclamation of the everlasting gospel and indeed we will see Jesus come soon to take us home.

General Conference Youth Ministries Department

Why This Book?

Dear Young Preacher,

You hold our hearts in your hand right now, believe us. We know that it may look like a book, but this is no ordinary book. It is a labor of love and a treasure trove of biblical truth and beauty. Our blood, sweat, and tears of joy are in these sermons. We're asking you to hold these sermons—this work of heart—close to your own heart.

Why should you?

Not just because they are dear to us, but far more importantly because they hold the very truths that are dearest to the heart of God Himself! These twelve sermons are about The One, Jesus Christ. Like all good sermons, these seek to lift Him higher and higher in the minds and hearts of the readers and hearers.

The concept behind *The One* is that Jesus Christ is revealed in Scripture as multidimensional in His various saving roles. He is Creator. And King. And Savior. And Healer. And more. He is The One, but like a multihued and multifaceted diamond, He is beautiful, and yet, a little different from every angle. These sermons seek to explore some of the most illuminating and incandescent truths about His person, character, and ministry. And yet, after these thousands of words have been written and spoken, we've only begun to scratch the surface.

These sermons have been written in partnership with the General Conference of Seventh-day Adventist's Youth Ministries Department, under the directorship of Pastor Gilbert Cangy. From the beginning, Gilbert's vision was that these sermons would be thoroughly Christ-centered and also thoroughly Adventist. Fortunately, this is no difficult task, since the Adventist message is, by nature, so grandly, beautifully, and completely centered in Jesus Christ. Thank you, Pastor Gilbert, for your vision and passion for both the truth and the youth!

Oh, and do not forget to let your pastor know what you're up to. He/she will be glad, no doubt, to support you in any way they can. Ask them for advice and for prayer. Your pastor should be your biggest asset in essential preparations, so stay close to him/her.

This is the first of a two-part series. We'll be releasing another sermon series in about a year, so be on the lookout for it. It will delve into the great prophecies of Scripture and take a serious and sober look at the terrible, tragic, and tricky times in which we live. So after you've preached these sermons once or twice (or even more), get ready for round two!

On the next page you will find some tips and encouragement to get you fired up. Now get out there and have fun because honestly, and believe us on this, there is nothing more enjoyable, fulfilling, challenging, and just plain awesome than telling people about Jesus Christ.

Now, get up front and...preach your guts out!

He is The One!

Your friends,

David Asscherick and Ty Gibson

HELPFUL TIPS from Ty and David

- Get up there—wherever "there" is: a church, a town hall, a gymnasium, a rented auditorium, a school room, a living room, an open field, or any other place where you can get a crowd, whether great or small, together. Yes, get up in front and . . . preach your guts out!

- Between the two of us, we've preached thousands of sermons, and the best sermons are always those that you put your whole heart, soul, and enthusiasm into. Don't be afraid or ashamed or embarrassed. Just be yourself for Jesus! He will stand with you as you seek to lift Him up before the people.

- You can have confidence in these sermons, trust us. They are solidly biblical and squarely Christ-centered. So preach with confidence and conviction!

- Sure, there are other little pieces of homiletical advice we could give. After nearly forty years of combined preaching, we've learned a few things. But you know what? Like swimming, the best way to learn is to just get in the water and do it. Sure, you may make a mistake or two (or three or more!). Sure, you may swallow some water and feel like you're going to drown. But you won't. You'll learn, you'll grow, and you'll be better for it in the end.

- These sermons are written in manuscript form. You could, if you wanted, just stand up and read them as is. A better way to do it, though, is to read the sermon over and over and over again.

Look up each of the texts and read them again and again. Let the presentation soak into your mind. Read it aloud so your mouth gets accustomed to saying the words and phrases.

- Use the margins. Make your own notes and write your own stories and illustrations in the margins. These sermons will be best when you take the time to make them your own. Think of them as a skeleton. Yes, they are complete and stable as is, but they'll be better yet when you lay your own muscle, sinew, and skin over them.

- If you want, practice preaching them in the garage, in front of a mirror, or to your cat or cousin. This will help you feel comfortable when the time comes to give it your all.

- Pray. Before you stand up to preach, be sure you kneel down to pray. The greatest preachers have always been, first and foremost, great Christians. And great Christians know from experience the power and practice of prayer. So be sure you're prayed up and connected to Jesus Christ. Confess your sins, your insecurities, your doubts and fears. Open up to Him; it's that openness with God that will allow you to truly open up to others. Your power will come from your connection to Christ, and your connection to Christ is tied directly to prayer. So before you preach your guts out, be sure to pray your knees off. Well, maybe not off, but you get the point.

THE MAKER

THE COMMUNICATOR

THE KING

THE SAVIOR

THE SPIRIT

THE GREAT GIVER

THE HEALER

THE SACRIFICE

THE NEW MAN

THE MESSENGER

THE BRIDEGROOM

THE BODY

01. THE MAKER
the character of God

BIBLE TEXT: In the beginning God created the heavens and the earth. (Genesis 1:1)

PRESENTER'S NOTE: On page 26 you will need to insert a personal story about a relationship you enjoy. Something like, "I've been married to my best friend for __ years. . ." Or, "I totally enjoy spending time with my son. . ." Or, "Every time I see a friend of mine named _____, I feel alive . . . and the happiness I feel when I'm with her/him reflects the very fabric of reality as God intended it to be. It tells me something about the heart of God and draws me to Him." **Prepare your story ahead of time.**

the **MAKER** synopsis

The first name given to God in Scripture, Elohim, shows that God is a plurality of being. The Bible also defines God as love. If love is the opposite of self-seeking, then God, in His very nature, is a plurality of personhood, a social unit of Father, Son, and Spirit who exist as one beautiful, relational reality. Creation was born of the outpouring of that divine, creative love. Throughout our lives that primal love calls to us. God's love is the foundational meaning of our existence and defines who and what we are as human beings.

The Maker

It would be very odd if I were to introduce myself to you in the plural: "Hello! My name is (_____ presenter's name here, in the plural)."

You might whisper to the person sitting next to you, "Is he crazy? Does he think there's more than one of him?" And you'd be right to wonder about my sanity, or at least about my grasp of singular versus plural grammar. As you can plainly see, there is only one of me. I'm not (_____ presenter's name here, in the plural). I'm (_____ presenter's name, singular). I am a single, solitary person. A plural identification of myself would make no sense at all.

And yet—strangely, or not so strangely, as we will see—this is exactly how the Maker of the universe is introduced to us the first time we encounter Him in Scripture. Look at the opening sentence of the Bible:

> In the beginning God created the heavens and the earth. (Genesis 1:1)

Most translations read as this one does: "In the beginning God…"

But that's too generic. It would be like me introducing myself to you by saying, "Hello! I'm human," to which you might respond, "Um, okay, I'm human too," while wondering if I'm a little, or a lot, weird.

In the original language, which was Hebrew, it's not merely "God," as if some general, non-specific notion of deity is being declared. Rather, it's a kind of name.

"In the beginning Elohim…"

Ah, now we're getting acquainted. Here we encounter a specific God identified by a specific name.

So, the name is Elohim. But this is no ordinary name. In fact, it's a peculiar kind of name, but also very enlightening: peculiar because it is a plural noun, enlightening because it contains the secret truth of God's own essential identity.

The use of Elohim informs us that God is a plurality of being, not a strict singularity of being. God is one and yet more than one. God is both self and other within the sacred parameters of the divine nature.

What this means, in the most practical sense, is this:

God is a social unit.

A relational dynamic.

A family.

A friendship.

Scripture employs a crucially important word to encapsulate this core reality about God. In fact, it would be impossible to overstate the importance of the use of this word. In 1 John 4:8 we read the three most powerful and illuminating words we can ever know or speak:

"God is love."

Believe it or not, this simple yet profound declaration tells us the whole truth about God.

The whole truth, and nothing but the truth!

Notice it does not merely say, God is loving (an adjective), nor God loves (a verb), but rather, God is love (a noun). In other words, the statement, "God is love," defines God's total identity, character, and personhood. Everything else that is true of God is true of God because God is love. Said another way, all the attributes that compose God's character are extensions of the fact the God is love.

For example, the Bible never says, God is justice, but rather that God is just. Never that God is mercy, but rather that God is merciful. God is just precisely because He is love. God is merciful due to the fact that He is love. Both justice and mercy are dimensions of God's love, and the same is true of all other divine attributes. Not one of them is different than or contrary to God's love.

So, then, it is vital that we understand what Scripture means by the word "love," because once we define love we will know precisely who and what manner of person God is.

Scripture leaves us with no ambiguity as to what love is. Turn to 1 Corinthians 13. We'll begin in verse 4:

Love suffers long and is kind; love does not envy; love does not parade itself, is not puffed up; [5]does not behave rudely, does not seek its own, is not provoked, thinks no evil; [6]does not rejoice in iniquity, but rejoices in the truth; [7]bears all things, believes all things, hopes all things, endures all things. [8]Love never fails.

Brilliant!

The apostle Paul here tells us what love looks like in action, and by so doing he tells us what God looks like in action. Since "God is love," we could also read the passage like this:

God suffers long and is kind; God does not envy; God does not parade Himself, is not puffed up; [5] God does not behave rudely, does not seek His own, is not provoked, thinks no evil; [6]God does not rejoice in iniquity, but rejoices in the truth; [7]God bears all things, believes all things, hopes all things, endures all things. [8]God never fails.

What a beautiful, amazing picture!

So then, if we were to summarize what love is, and therefore what kind of person God is, what would be the basic idea? With this biblical definition of love before us, we would say:

God is self-giving. Or, God is other-centered.

Now, think something through with me, something very important. In order for love to exist, there must be someone to love. Simple, right? So, if God is love, and love is not self-seeking, then it is evident that God, in His very nature, is a plurality of personhood, a social unit of divine persons who exist as one beautiful, relational reality.

This is why Scripture identifies God as three persons who collectively compose one God: God the Father, God the Son, and God the Holy Spirit. Realizing from Scripture's testimony that God consists of Father, Son, and Holy Spirit living eternally in self-giving love for one another, the early church coined the word Trinity to describe this sublime reality. While the word Trinity itself does not occur in Scripture, the truth of God as three eternal persons is clearly and beautifully evident throughout.

One example is Paul's closing salutation to the Corinthian church in which he identifies the personhood of all three members of the Trinity as a blessing upon the believers:

The grace of the Lord Jesus Christ, and the love of God, and the communion of the Holy Spirit be with you all. (2 Corinthians 13:14)

Another translation renders the blessing this way:

> The amazing grace of the Master, Jesus Christ, the extravagant love of God, the intimate friendship of the Holy Spirit, be with all of you. (The Message)

If God were a strict singularity, a solitary person, it could not be said with any rational coherence that "God is love." As we have already highlighted, love cannot exist in a state of isolation. In order for love to be an active reality, there must be someone besides oneself to love.

This point is well made by engaging in a little conversational exercise. I'll ask a series of questions, and you answer according to what you think the answer would be from Scripture.

Is the Father God?

Yes.

But is the Father all there is of God?

No.

Is the Son, Jesus Christ, God?

Yes.

But is Jesus all there is of God?

No.

Is the Holy Spirit God?

Yes.

But is the Holy Spirit all there is of God?

No.

So then, together, all three compose one divine reality.

Regarding the relationship that Father, Son, and Holy Spirit bear one to another, Scripture says:

> There are three that bear witness in heaven: the Father, the Word, and the Holy Spirit; and these three are one. (1 John 5:7)

The Gospel of John tells us that Jesus came to our world from "the bosom of the Father" (John 1:18), meaning that before His incarnation He existed in intimate friendship with the Father.

Speaking of His relationship with the Father, Jesus said:

> I and My Father are one. (John 10:30)

Expanding the idea of their oneness, in an intimate moment of prayer to the Father, Jesus said:

> You loved Me before the foundation of the world. (John 17:24)

In one Old Testament prophecy about Jesus' coming to earth as our Savior, God the Father calls Him, "My Elect One in whom My soul delights" (Isaiah 42:1), and in another passage, "the Man who is My Companion" (Zechariah 13:7).

A more beautiful picture of God cannot be imagined. For all eternity past, God the Father, God the Son, and God the Holy Spirit existed together as Elohim, the three who are one, living in self-giving, other-centered love for one another, delighting in one another's companionship. It is an astounding thing to realize that there lies at the foundation of reality an enjoyable, happy friendship. This is what Scripture means when it says, "God is love."

But that's not the end of the story! In a way, it's just the beginning—literally!—because from the beauty of divine love, creation was born.

Let me say that again: from the beauty of divine love, creation was born!

Turn in your Bible once more to the opening declaration of Genesis:

> In the beginning God created the heavens and the earth. (Genesis 1:1)

And then go down to verses 26 and 27:

> Then God said, 'Let Us make man in Our image, according to Our likeness.' . . . So God created man in His own image; in the image of God He created him; male and female He created them.

Notice that, according to the passages, God's passion is to create, and notice further that personal beings made in "His own image" are the pinnacle expression of His creative power and passion. This makes such perfect sense. If God is love, and if love is all about others, it logically—and again, beautifully!—follows that God would want to create others.

"And why," someone might ask, "would He want to do that?"

Well, isn't it obvious? So He can love them! So the same love that exists between Father, Son, and Spirit might be replicated in the living experience of others.

Astounding!

Wonderful!

Beautiful!

Our Maker made us to love us, to live for us, to engage in relationship with us, and, by logical extension, He made us so that we might love one another as well.

We might even read Genesis 1:1 like this:

> In the beginning Love created the heavens and the earth.

It is the reality of God's personal, other-centered love that gave us existence as human beings, as people, moms, dads, children, brothers, sisters, and friends.

Pause to let the thought register: you exist as the from and for of God's love.

Now then, let's loop back into the Creation story for some expanded detail to fill in our picture of God and our relationship to Him.

So much of God's friendly personality and loving character come through in the biblical record of Creation. As the account unfolds in Genesis one and two, we see Him moving about, shaping and arranging the pieces of an emerging work of art.

> God created...God moved upon...God called...God made...God divided...God gathered together...God formed...God breathed. (Genesis 1 and 2)

Divine love is here demonstrated as the out-flowing of creative energy into the making of beautiful things for others to enjoy.

There is light, composed of a full spectrum of radiant colors.

There is water, shimmering in the light, swelling, descending, flowing, reflecting.

There is the firmament, the visible arc of the sky mirroring the rich, blended colors of "the earth" and "the sea."

The sky is studded with two great lights and a multitude of stars.

The waters abound with an abundance of living creatures, of every shape and color imaginable.

Impossibly colorful and graceful birds glide across the face of the firmament of the heavens, bringing pleasure, wonder, and delight. Living creatures walk and hop and plod and roll and bound and scurry and run over land covered with lush vegetation. Some are of solemn appearance to arouse deep contemplation. Some are apparently deliberately funny to prompt laughter. Some are majestic beyond description to awaken a sense of utter amazement.

As the living, fluid masterpiece takes on form and feature, the One who is the Maker speaks words of satisfaction at the creative expressions flowing from His eager heart: "God saw that it was good...good...good...good...good...very good" (Genesis 1 and 2).

Meaning what, exactly?

Certainly it is functional as a system. But mere functionality is not what the Creator has in mind, though functionality is vital to His purpose. He is more than an engineer; He is an artist with a lover's heart. It is fascinating, then, but not surprising, that the Hebrew word *tomb*, here simply translated "good," has a much richer meaning: "Beautiful, bountiful, cheerful, fair, fine, joyful, kindly, loving, pleasant, wealthy" (Strong's Concordance). The creation is "good" in the sense that it is boundlessly rich with the capacity to impart pleasure.

And why?

Why such extravagance and attention to detail?

Well, why else?

Because it is all a gift of love!

True to His heart, true to His selfless and giving identity, God created the earth and all its wonders for others. He is the One,

> "Who created the heavens,
>
> Who is God,
>
> Who formed the earth and made it,
>
> Who has established it,
>
> Who did not create it in vain,
>
> Who formed it to be inhabited" (Isaiah 45:18).

Once all was ready, "Then God said, 'Let Us make man in Our image'."

The Genesis record shows God, the Artistic Lover, reaching the crescendo of His work by creating living beings as recipients of all He had made. They are unique among the vast scope of created things in that they are conscious persons who are capable of noticing their surroundings and experiencing the pleasures those surroundings afford. They are the final act of Creation and—don't miss this point!—all that was made before them was crafted with them in mind.

That's right, all along Creation was going somewhere, to someone!

> The Lord has been mindful of us . . . Who made heaven and earth. The heaven,
> even the heavens, are the Lord's; but the earth He has given to the children of men.
> (Psalm 115:12, 15-16)

Imagine Adam and Eve awaking to their first few moments of life. How delighted they must have been to open their eyes and look into the intensely passionate eyes of their Maker. Everything that greeted their newly formed senses excited joy and pleasure. Having given them the gift of life itself, God immediately proceeded to lavish additional gifts upon them.

First, "God blessed them" (Genesis 1:28).

I can imagine the blessing may have gone something like this:

> "Welcome to life. This is the world I have made for you. I am your Creator. I have cherished the thought of you for a long time. Now, finally, your time has come.

You are alive—so perfect, so very good and beautiful. Look around you. Listen to the lovely sounds. All of this is for you, from Me. I love you."

He gave them the gift of dominion, which means they were free to cultivate their impressionable environment and be creative:

> Be fruitful and multiply; fill the earth and subdue it; have dominion over… every living thing. (Genesis 1:28)

He gave them the gift of tasty, nourishing food to eat:

> God said, 'See, I have given you every herb that yields seed which is on the face of all the earth, and every tree whose fruit yields seed; to you it shall be for food.' (Genesis 1:29)

> And out of the ground the Lord God made every tree to grow that is pleasant to the sight and good for food. The tree of life was also in the midst of the garden. (Genesis 2:9)

He gave them one another, the gift of companionship, sexuality, and the remarkable ability to procreate in their own blended image:

> [God] made . . . a woman, and He brought her to the man. (Genesis 2:22)

> Male and female He created them . . . and God said to them 'Be fruitful and multiply.' (Genesis 1:27-28)

> They shall become one flesh. (Genesis 2:24)

He gave them a special garden home that He Himself had planted. While the earth, as a whole, remained something of a wilderness that they were to have the privilege of subduing into a beautiful system of order, there was one spot that was perfected for them by God's own hands:

> The Lord God planted a garden eastward in Eden, and there He put the man whom He had formed. (Genesis 2:8)

Eden actually means "pleasure," a name signifying God's intention for the couple. Adam and Eve were to live and love with extreme pleasure by the Creator's design. All of their senses—sight, hearing, touch, taste, and smell—were continually flooded with holy, pleasure-inducing stimuli.

We find the story of Genesis so attractive and believable because we sense, deep inside, that we belong to that story, that we were made for that kind of painless, blissful place, free from all evil and pain. Every time we see beauty or experience love, it's as if we're amnesia victims getting little memory flashes of who we really are.

Eden calls us.

The biblical picture of Creation, and the God of Creation, drives us to an astounding and delightful realization: If God's love is the matrix from whence we came to be, then God's love must be the meaning of our existence. Love, as it occurs within the fellowship of the Trinity, is the social blueprint that defines who and what we are as human beings, or at least what we're supposed to be.

The alternative view of human origins is a study in extreme contrast. Atheistic materialism says that human beings are the product of a chaotic and mindless process of evolutionary chance. In this worldview, life has no intrinsic or transcendent meaning. We're born, we fulfill our biological urges, we die, and that's it. There is no actual worth to any human being and no real value in life other than whatever an individual can grab and gulp before death. There is no God and there is no moral dimension to reality—no truly good or bad, truly right or wrong.

And this nagging desire for love we all feel? Well, it's an illusion we've somehow concocted in our collective imaginations, because in the evolutionary framework there is no such thing as love as an eternal, beautiful feature of reality. No, the highest law of life is self-preservation or, as it's been called, the "survival of the fittest."

So what is a human being in this view? Merely an evolving animal governed by self-preserving instincts and destined for eventual extinction.

It is difficult to imagine a more bleak view of life and reality.

The biblical account of human origins says that "God is love" in the most amazing, beautiful, and meaningful sense imaginable, and that this God "made man in His own image." This worldview—which just means, this way of viewing the world—imparts dignity and worth to men and women. It tells us we were made to be something noble and great and wonderful. It answers to our voracious hunger for meaning, for significance, and for purpose. It tells us that the reason we long for love is because we were mentally, emotionally, and even biologically engineered for love by a God whose very nature is love.

The Creation account of Scripture and the modern myth of atheistic evolution are two diametrically opposed views of reality. The first is fundamentally about love, while the second is fundamentally about selfishness.

Let me repeat that: the first is fundamentally about love, while the second is fundamentally about selfishness.

Now, what does your heart, deep down, tell you is true? Which view of reality more accords with your deepest longings and your most intuitive sense of what life is really all about? And, really, which view is worth living for?

As long as you live.

No matter where you are.

Or what you're doing.

Or what mistakes you've made.

Or what successes you've had.

No matter what, never forget your Maker.

Never, ever, ever forget that God is love.

It is the truest and most beautiful thing you will ever know.

My appeal to you, and to myself, is that we would acknowledge the God of Scripture as our Maker and embrace His love as the real meaning, purpose, and beauty of life. Is that, dear friend, your desire?

Insert your story here. Instructions on page 15

PRESENTER, PLEASE SHARE WITH YOUR AUDIENCE THAT THIS IS A SAFE ZONE.
It's a safe place to be themselves. • Everyone has the right to their own opinion.
There are no dumb questions. • All comments are encouraged and respected.

Discussion Questions

1. In what ways have you tried to define or understand the three-in-one nature of the Godhead?

2. What problems do you have with this concept?

3. The lesson predicates God's plurality, in part, on the principle that love cannot exist without someone to love. Do you agree or disagree, and why?

4. What is your reaction to the passage that describes God as being just, not justice, being merciful, not mercy, and of those things being part of the love that God is?

5. How does it make you feel to think of your unique self as having been born of the outpouring of divine love? How does it make you feel to think of yourself as having been born of a random combination of atoms?

6. What are some of the problems that have arisen over the millennia from the idea that the earth was created "for us"?

7. What might you say and do to help others consider the earth as a loving gift to be cared for rather than a "thing" to dominate, use up, and throw away?

8. What is your reaction to this passage? "Every time we see beauty or experience love, it's as if we're amnesia victims getting little memory flashes of who we really are. Eden calls us."

9. What could you do to more fully immerse yourself in God's love—to belong to, live in, and more deeply experience this divine love and joy?

THE MAKER

THE COMMUNICATOR

THE KING

THE SAVIOR

THE SPIRIT

THE GREAT GIVER

THE HEALER

THE SACRIFICE

THE NEW MAN

THE MESSENGER

THE BRIDEGROOM

THE BODY

02. COMMUNICATOR
love and self-revelation

BIBLE TEXT: No longer do I call you servants, for a servant does not know what his master is doing; but I have called you friends, for all things that I heard from My Father I have made known to you. (John 15:15)

PRESENTER'S NOTE:
- Read. Read. Read.
- Let this message soak into your mind.
- Take the time to make it your own.

Review all the discussion questions early.

the COMMUNICATOR synopsis

Our strong inclination to speak and be spoken to reflects the fact that a communicating God is the matrix of our origins. The Bible claims to be God's word to humanity. There are at least four sets of evidence for this claim: 1) A God of love would, by definition, communicate with the loved ones; 2) the story the Bible tells makes rational sense, emotional sense, moral sense, and relational sense; 3) the foretelling prophecies of the Bible come true; and 4) it exerts a transforming impact on the lives of those who believe its revelations. After we realize the first three lines of evidence are true, then the Bible actually challenges us to put it to the test, to act upon its claims and see if we don't experience the transformation of heart and life that it promises.

The Communicator

Have you noticed that our world is engaged in a full-on communication frenzy?

Sure you have, and you are undoubtedly part of it to some degree, as am I. Here are some numbers that will no doubt have already grown by the time you hear or read this:

Sixty billion emails are sent each day.

More than one billion people are now active on Facebook. That's one out of every seven people on the planet, while five million new users are signing up each week.

Twitter has five hundred million active users, generating more than 340 million messages per day. Yes, that's *per day*.

In a world of seven billion people, there are six billion activated cell phone subscriptions. And Africa, once largely off the communications grid, is now the second largest cell phone market with more than 600 million users.

Text messaging is by far the most popular form of communication. Roughly 200,000 text messages are sent every second, more than 1.5 trillion every year. The Philippines alone sends an average of 400 million text messages per day, or approximately 142 billion per year.

Everyone has something to say.

But why?

Well, I suppose because everyone wants to be heard!

Yes, but why?

Well, because everyone wants to be understood.

Okay, but why?

Because—bottom line—everyone wants to be loved.

Ah, now we're getting to the real heart of the matter.

Human beings are hungry for contact because we're hungry for love. Communication is in our DNA because we are mentally, emotionally, and even biologically engineered for love. We are communicators by nature because we are, by nature, relational beings. We want to know others and to be known by them.

It should come as no surprise to us, then, that God, too, is a communicator. After all, we were made in His image, as we discovered in our first message. Our strong inclination to speak and be spoken to reflects the fact that a communicating God is the matrix of our origins.

The Bible makes the astounding claim about itself that it is God's communication device, God's own "word." For example, the apostle Paul says in 2 Timothy 3:16:

> All Scripture is given by inspiration of God.

No question about it, this is a bold and audacious claim. Essentially Paul is saying that the ideas conveyed in the pages of Scripture are "God-breathed," that they have their origin in the mind and will of the One who made the universe.

The apostle Peter makes the same claim in 2 Peter 1:20-21:

> …knowing this first, that no prophecy of Scripture is of any private interpretation, for prophecy never came by the will of man, but holy men of God spoke as they were moved by the Holy Spirit.

Now think about it: if this claim is true, then we have in our possession the most priceless treasure of knowledge and insight imaginable. If it's not true, well then, we have before us the most persuasive and outlandish hoax in history.

So the natural question, then, is this: How can we know whether the claim of Scripture to be God's word is true? I'd like you to consider with me four lines of evidence in favor of the claim:

1. The logic of love
2. The self-evident truth-quality of the biblical storyline
3. Bible prophecy
4. Personal experience

Let's explore all four points.

Okay, number one is what I'm calling the "logic of love." The reasoning goes like this:

a. If God exists, and

b. If God is a personal being whose essential character is love (discoveries we made in our first message), then it logically follows that

c. God is a communicator.

Why?

Because it is in the nature of love to be relationally engaged, and communication is the means by which relational engagement occurs.

Said another way, persons who are motivated by love for others go out of their way to proactively communicate with those they love. So because God is a personal being of other-centered love, as we discovered in our first message, then we would expect God to go out of His way to intentionally communicate with us in a coherent manner. And the most coherent way to communicate, of course, is with words. So then, once one believes in the existence of a personal God, it is the most logical thing in the world to believe that this God would provide some source of God-inspired words.

Jesus wrapped language around this idea. Open your Bible to John 15:15. Notice how Jesus describes the kind of relationship He wants with us, and notice the means by which He seeks to facilitate the relationship:

> No longer do I call you servants, for a servant does not know what his master is doing; but I have called you friends, for all things that I heard from My Father I have made known to you.

Be sure to get these two points:

1. The relationship God wants with us is friendship.

2. The means He will pursue to facilitate that relationship is to make things known to us, that is, by means of communication.

This is really quite amazing. Here is the most powerful Being in existence, God incarnate, the Almighty Creator of the Universe, and He says "I don't want you to be My servants, but rather My friends." If anyone could force us into submission and get away with it, God could. And yet, He simply chooses not to. There is something inherent in God's very makeup that excludes dominance and precludes silence.

The master-servant relationship is characterized by ignorance and fear. The servant does what he's told because he's told, not because he knows the master's thinking and agrees with the plan. Knowing and agreeing is irrelevant to the master-slave arrangement. Friendship, on the other hand, is characterized by understanding, trust, and love. As friends of God, He invites us into His thoughts, His feelings, His motives. He wants us to think, to know, and to freely choose. And so, with friendship as His desire, He says, "all things that I heard from My Father I have made known to you." In other words, I will communicate with you.

King David prayed to God the prayer of a friend:

> Give me understanding, and I shall keep Your Law; indeed, I shall observe it with my whole heart. (Psalm 119:34)

Notice that there is a direct link for David between understanding (the rational action of the mind) and obedience (the voluntary action of the will). He realizes that if God increases His comprehension, he will be motivationally empowered to render a more intelligent and wholehearted obedience.

By giving us sacred writings—words that accurately communicate His mind—God is basically saying, I want you to understand rather than be controlled. I respect the dignity of your rational, free humanity. I want you to know Me and, if you like what you see, I invite you to live in harmony with Me as your Maker.

The Scriptures are an expression of God's respect for the human race and His desire to preserve our freedom rather than subsume our individuality within His own. He would rather love us than dominate us. So then, our first line of evidence in favor of the Bible as the word of God is the logic of love.

Our second line of evidence is—note the language carefully—the self-evident truth-quality of the biblical storyline. This point naturally flows out of our first line of evidence, because the logic of love is precisely what forms the narrative of Scripture.

The idea here is this: the story told in Scripture just happens to interface perfectly with reality as we experience it—like hand to glove, shoe to foot, male to female. When we hear what Scripture has to say about our origins and our ultimate destiny, our moral condition and its remedy, the meaning of our lives and what happens when we die, we find that the story makes rational sense, emotional sense, moral sense, and relational sense. Another way of saying this is that the story of Scripture rings intuitively true.

In the briefest manner, allow me to tell you the story of Scripture.

In the beginning God created the heavens and the earth, and He created humankind in His own image. This is how the story of Scripture begins. It rings true because it bestows dignity upon the human being. Our natural sense of rage against all injustice, prejudice, and oppression is the outgrowth of our deeply ingrained sense that we are more than mere animals on an evolutionary quest for self-preservation.

The story of Scripture continues by informing us that human beings, while originally created in the image of God, have become morally fallen, selfish, rebellious, and filled with shame and guilt because of that fallenness. This part of the biblical story rings true because all of us as human beings experience guilt in our consciousness due to our failures to live with relational integrity.

And then the story of Scripture presents to us precisely the kind of Savior that we know we need. Unlike any other religion, philosophy, or self-help technique that has ever been conceived, the biblical narrative says that what we need is grace, free forgiveness from a God of unconditional love. This part of the story rings true because we all know that we need forgiveness and we all long for a love that finds no perfectly satisfying match in this world.

The story of Scripture makes rational sense because the things it tells us about ourselves and reality as a whole resonate with our sense that humanity comes from an elevated origin from which we have fallen. It is our innate sense that all human beings are of supreme value and share a status of equality.

It makes moral sense because its most simple declarations of right and wrong, good and evil, find resonance in the human conscience. The moral standard held out in Scripture, simply put, is love.

And it makes relational sense because it tells us that we are physically, emotionally, and psychologically made for relationships of integrity with God and our fellow human beings.

In the narrative of Scripture the deepest and most persistent needs of the human being are met. Thus, the Bible bears testimony to its supernatural origin.

This brings us to our third point—Bible prophecy. In brief, the point is this: if the Bible is the inspired word of God, then we would expect it to possess certain unmistakable characteristics that demonstrate its divinely-inspired nature. And that is precisely what we do find. Scripture bears internal witness to its inspired quality by doing something truly amazing and persuasive—by foretelling the future with perfect accuracy.

Let's briefly consider just one of the many instances of Bible prophecy.

In Scripture we encounter the astounding fact that multiple prophets, spanning hundreds of years, foretold various details concerning Jesus Christ. These are called Messianic prophecies. The Old Testament was written by some thirty-five to forty Hebrew prophets between about 1450 BC and 430 BC. Imbedded within its many stories, poems, songs, and visions are hundreds of prophecies about the coming Messiah. These prophecies specified many aspects of His Messianic mission including His incarnation, the place of His birth, the specific time of His public ministry, the time of His death, the manner of His death, and the revolutionary impact He would have upon the world.

Here are several examples:

1. The prophet Micah foretold that the Messiah would be born in Bethlehem (Micah 5:2), which Jesus was (Matthew 2:1-2).

2. Isaiah foretold that the Messiah would be heralded by a forerunner figure crying out in the wilderness. This was fulfilled in the ministry of John the Baptist (Isaiah 40:3-9; John 1:19-34).

3. Zechariah foretold that the Messiah would enter into the city of Jerusalem as a king riding on a donkey (Zechariah 9:9), and Jesus did this (Matthew 21:1-11).

4. Zechariah foretold that the Messiah would be betrayed into the hands of His enemies by a friend and suffer wounds in His hands (Zechariah 13:6). This is precisely what happened (Matthew 26:49-50).

5. Zechariah also foretold that the Messiah would be betrayed for thirty pieces of silver (Zechariah 11:12). This is, again, precisely what happened (Matthew 26:15).

6. And that the money would be used to buy a potter's field (Zechariah 11:13), which was fulfilled (Matthew 27:5-7).

7. Isaiah foretold that the Messiah would remain silent while suffering abuse (Isaiah 53:7). Jesus displayed exactly this attitude (Matthew 27:12-14).

8. King David foretold that the Messiah would die by having His hands and feet pierced (Psalm 22:16). This, too, is what happened (Luke 23:33).

Now think about the chances that all of these prophecies could be fulfilled in the life of one person. And the list could go on. There are more than 400 such messianic prophecies, and Jesus fulfilled them all. But let's just apply some math to the eight we've listed. What are the chances that all of these eight prophecies would be fulfilled, by mere chance or happenstance, in one person?

Probability theory is a branch of mathematics that applies the science of math to the probability of any given phenomenon. This is how it works: A single prediction with only two possible outcomes has a fifty percent chance of being fulfilled. If a second prediction is made concerning the same person or event, the law of compound probability comes into play. The chances of two predictions being fulfilled concerning one person or event, each with only two possible outcomes, is twenty-five percent, or one chance in four. With each additional prediction concerning the same person or event, the fraction of probability lessens. If you add the factor that there are more than two possible outcomes for each of the predicted events, the fraction of probability diminishes exponentially.

Now then, the Old Testament has many such prophecies concerning the coming, character, and career of the Messiah. But if we only consider the eight prophecies we've just delineated, the chances of one man fulfilling these prophecies would be ten to the 28th power–that's a ten followed by twenty-eight zeroes! In other words, a very, very large number and, thus, virtually impossible.

To put this in perspective, imagine someone predicting that the 68th president of the United States will be born in Riverside, CA. If that single prediction came true, that would be amazing enough. But what if additional predictions were added? Not only will the 68th president of the United States be born in Riverside, CA, he will begin his presidency in 2030, and then three and a half years into his presidency he will be assassinated, and the assassination will be carried out with a .22 caliber handgun, by one of his close political allies. Now we have moved beyond the realm of amazing into the realm of impossible. There is simply no way that all of these converging features could be foretold years in advance and then be fulfilled without foreknowledge.

The prophesies concerning Jesus Christ are so specific, with such a number of distinct features given, that, apart from divine foreknowledge, the probability of fulfillment as a matter of accidental coincidence is reduced to a fraction too small to comprehend.

Our fourth line of evidence in favor of the Bible as the word of God is the witness of personal experience.

The gist of this point is that the Bible gives evidence of its claim to be the word of God by the transforming impact it exerts on the lives of those who believe its revelations. Yes, this point is subjective. It constitutes a bold challenge that can only be put to the test by the individual. Certainly the subjective nature of this point would render it suspect if the first three lines of evidence proved false. But it is a wholly rational move to put Scripture to the test in your own experience in the light of the first three lines of evidence we have just explored.

Jesus said it this way in John 7:17:

> If any man will do His will, he shall know of the doctrine, whether it be of God, or whether I speak of myself.

Essentially Jesus is saying here that any person who proceeds with faith to act upon the word of God will recognize its veracity in the very process of the doing.

The apostle John explains this concept with greater detail in 1 John 5:9-13:

> If we receive the witness of men, the witness of God is greater; for this is the witness of God which He has testified of His Son. He who believes in the Son of God has the witness in himself; he who does not believe God has made Him a liar, because he has not believed the testimony that God has given of His Son. And this is the testimony: that God has given us eternal life, and this life is in His Son. He who has the Son has life; he who does not have the Son of God does not have life. These things I have written to you who believe in the name of the Son of God, that you may know that you have eternal life, and that you may continue to believe in the name of the Son of God.

Three points stand out here:

1. John says that it is common for us to believe the witness of human beings and act upon what they tell us. Then he challenges us to act upon the witness of God, which is, he says, greater.

2. If we will do so, John says that a phenomenon of realization will occur within us. We will experience the witness of the truth of Christ within our own heart, mind, and life. Sure, it's a mystery, but it's also awesome. Trust me.

3. His final point is that once we receive the witness of God through Christ, we will obtain the internal sense of assurance that we have eternal life.

This is nothing short of astounding if you pause to really think about it. Scripture is basically challenging us to put it to the test, to act upon its claims and see if we don't experience the transformation of heart and life that it promises.

The genius of God revealing Himself with words in a book is that it allows us the perfect balance of freedom and evidence. It allows us to encounter God on the character level while remaining free from the overwhelming force of His immediate presence. This really is the best way for God to introduce Himself to us, even though we may, at times, think we would prefer a different method. The written word of Scripture is a creation of divine genius—a living, active, communicating medium that effectively unfolds God's identity. The necessity of approaching Him through a written revelation places us in the position of deeply pondering His character, allowing us to respond, again, unforced by the overpowering influence of His visible majesty. By giving us the Bible, God has shown Himself to be a gentleman, respectfully preserving our freedom to think through His claims and say yes or no without coercion.

In Scripture we are given sufficient evidence to believe, and yet left free to choose. We are invited to interact with its claims and promises and see whether the truthfulness of its witness rises within our awareness.

The sacred text of Scripture is the supremely practical communication tool God has chosen to facilitate our relationship with Him, granting us access to His heart and Him access to our hearts. God has some very important things to tell us and show us. There are things He wants you and me to know, things about our origins and why we exist, things about the meaning of life and how to live life to the full, how to cheat death and live forever, and most importantly how to experience the deep and personal realities of His love.

The Bible opens these subjects to our curious minds and to our relationally hungry hearts.

The question is, if you could interface with reality at its most intimate level, would you want to?

Would you cross that line?

Would you take the plunge?

Would you dare to know God if it were possible?

If your answer is yes, you will be pleased to know that this is the very experience Scripture holds out before you. You can know The One who is The Maker and discover Him to be The Communicator, as well, to your deepest heart of hearts. You are a personal being—so is God. You are a relational being—God is too. You long for intimacy—God is Himself the source of that longing inside of you. God wants you to be His friend, and communication is the means by which He intends to nurture our friendship with Him. Stated with utter simplicity, the reason we have the Bible is because God is love, and love, by its very nature, communicates. Why not put Him to the test? Why not take the Bible in hand and take it seriously? Why not explore its treasures and claim its promises? You have nothing to lose and everything to gain if it turns out that you find God speaking to you through its sacred pages, assuring you of His love and His gift of eternal life.

Yes, we are surrounded by a new explosion of information: texts, emails, Facebook messages, and more. But what if the most important message you've been sent isn't a modern electronic one, but an ancient spiritual one?

PRESENTER, PLEASE SHARE WITH YOUR AUDIENCE THAT THIS IS A SAFE ZONE.
It's a safe place to be themselves. • Everyone has the right to their own opinion. There are no dumb questions. • All comments are encouraged and respected.

Discussion Questions

1. What are the most frequent ways you communicate with others? What are the advantages and disadvantages of each?

2. Do you believe God communicates with people? What are some ways you might communicate with God?

3. Does the overall story of the Bible make "intuitive sense" to you? Are you familiar enough with it to say? How could you increase your familiarity?

4. What is your reaction to these passages? "There are more than 400 such messianic prophecies, and Jesus fulfilled them all . . . The chances of one man fulfilling these prophecies would be ten to the 28th power—that's a ten followed by twenty-eight zeroes!"

5. Share something someone told you that you trust to be true. How could you use that same sort of trust to try out the Scriptures?

6. What would change in your life if you set out to act as if the Bible were true in order to learn if it is so? What would you expect to happen?

THE MAKER

THE COMMUNICATOR

THE KING

THE SAVIOR

THE SPIRIT

THE GREAT GIVER

THE HEALER

THE SACRIFICE

THE NEW MAN

THE MESSENGER

THE BRIDEGROOM

THE BODY

03. THE KING

the law and government of God

BIBLE TEXT: Assuredly, I say to you that He will gird Himself and have them sit down to eat, and will come and serve them. (Luke 12:37)

PRESENTER'S NOTE:

· Read. Read. Read.

· Let this message soak into your mind.

· Take the time to make it your own.

  Review all the discussion questions early.

the KING synopsis

Power and humanity make an explosive combination. Yet in His humanity, Jesus completely upended the role of king and radically redefined what it meant to possess power. This message examines a)—Jesus' character: He stepped down from infinity to become a finite man, stooped down to touch the "untouchable" with love and compassion, then stepped down still further into a death by torture; b)—His government: unlike human systems, Jesus' upside-down government is one of eternal peace and utter wholeness; and c)—His law: the antithesis of human law, His is all about love—love God, love others as you love yourself. This King wants nothing more than a relationship with each of us.

The King

In 1884 something astounding happened in Naples, Italy.

The great cholera epidemic was taking lives by the thousands. But that was not the astounding thing. As bodies were piling up, those not infected sought isolation to protect themselves and caregivers were scarce. But that wasn't the astounding thing either. Into this dangerous situation, someone completely unexpected voluntarily showed up: the king himself, Umberto I. From bed to bed he visited the dying, touching them and speaking words of comfort, with no concern for himself. That was the astounding thing.

Apparently, there is more than one way to be king.

As a result of his selfless service, Umberto earned a name that few kings ever have. The common people of Italy called him, "The Good King."

Now it's important to recognize that there was a note of somber irony involved in bestowing this title, because while kings were common in history to that point, to be a good king was quite uncommon. If history teaches us anything at all, it teaches us that power is a precarious and dangerous thing in the hands of human beings. Reflecting on our world's long list of rulers, the historian, Lord Acton of England, offered this truism:

"Power tends to corrupt and absolute power corrupts absolutely."

The pharaohs declared themselves gods and built the Egyptian empire on the backs of slaves.

Alexander the Great became so drunk with power that conquest became a game he played to feed his ego.

The Caesars ruled the ever-expanding Roman Empire with ruthless cruelty, instilling terror in their subjects by employing horrific methods of public torture.

King Henry VIII used his power to riffle through wives like the courses of a French dinner, and then he founded the Church of England in order to evade accountability for his lust.

Lord Acton's truism seems to have few if any exceptions: "Power tends to corrupt and absolute power corrupts absolutely."

So it makes sense for human beings to be distrustful of kings and fearful of those who possess power. Powerful men have proven themselves to be self-serving with few exceptions. Even the apparently humble act of service King Umberto rendered to the cholera victims of Italy was overshadowed by his aspirations for colonization in Africa. When protests against his expansionist agenda arose in Milan, one of his generals opened canon fire on civilians, killing hundreds and wounding nearly a thousand, for which Umberto honored him.

Can anyone be trusted with power?

Can absolute power ever coexist with goodness of character?

Is there any king in whom we can put our confidence and not be disappointed?

The answer is yes, yes, and yes!

Scripture repeatedly confers upon Jesus the title of "king" while showing us how He completely upends the role and radically redefines what it means to possess power, to be king. Jesus is, in fact, the King we might legitimately call the Anti-King.

In order to sketch a profile of this One who is alone worthy to be King, we will allow Scripture to open our understanding to:

- His Character
- His Government
- His Law

Within the scope of these three profile points we will be asking and answering the simple and vital question, what kind of king is God revealed to be in Jesus Christ?

Let's go.

The Character of the King

To ponder the kingly character of Jesus is a study in contrasts because He is completely unlike what we generally expect in a king.

First of all, He acted out His kingly character by taking an infinite step down.

That's right—down!

He did this in the magnificent event we call "the incarnation." Paul stands blown away by the reality of the incarnation when he exclaims in 1 Timothy 3:16:

> Without controversy, great is the mystery of godliness: God was manifested in the flesh.

The incarnation of God in the man Christ Jesus constitutes the most astounding event ever to occur in all of universal history. This One—who is "in very nature God"—did not merely make a geographic journey from heaven to earth, but rather He made a metaphysical journey of nature. God literally became human. The word infinite comes to mind to describe the magnitude of this metamorphosis. This is not the caterpillar entering the cocoon and emerging the butterfly, but the butterfly entering the cocoon and emerging the caterpillar! The difference between being a human and being an earthworm is minuscule compared to what it would mean for the Almighty Creator of all material reality to become a human being. Illustrations fall flat to even approximate what it means for God to have become human.

But He did.

And yet, there is something about the incarnation we can comprehend. We can comprehend with intense wonder the character that was necessarily present in God that would move Him to voluntarily make such a monumental leap downward on our behalf. Let me say this clearly and slowly so as to impress it deeply upon us:

The incarnation reveals that God is self-giving in the most awesome sense imaginable.

But the incarnation was just the first step in this astounding display of self-giving love.

Once here among us in the flesh, Jesus manifested His kingly character by teaching the ignorant, healing the sick, tenderly touching the outcasts of society and forgiving the guilty. Every act of His life ministered to the needs of others. In every action and interaction, He announced the arrival of God's kingdom. Repeatedly He said, "The kingdom of God is at hand." Then He proceeded to demonstrate the principles of God's kingdom in living color for all to see and experience.

At last, King Jesus was enthroned in the most unlikely manner conceivable—upon an implement of torture, which His voluntary death transformed into a throne of glory.

Describing the paradox of the cross, Jesus said this:

> The hour has come that the Son of Man should be glorified. (John 12:23)

What?!

Glorified?!

How could dying on a cross as a tortured, humiliated victim of human injustice constitute being glorified? Earlier, in John chapter 10, verse 18, Jesus explained the secret glory of the cross:

> No one takes [My life] from Me, but I lay it down of Myself.

That's where the glory resides—in the fact that His death was a voluntary act of self-giving love. He was never powerless. His back was never up against a wall with no way out. Remember what He told Peter in Gethsemane:

> Do you think that I cannot now pray to My Father, and He will provide Me with more than twelve legions of angels? (Matthew 26:53)

The glory of the cross lies in its display of humility and love as the true power of the one true King.

Now, make no mistake about it, Jesus is powerful in the extreme. He is the almighty Creator of the universe. But also make no mistake about this: He rules by love alone. If Jesus wanted to rule over us with sheer brute force, He could. And yet, the most powerful being in the universe, the only being who could dominate us with unmatchable force and be answerable to no one other than Himself, doesn't want to.

Why?

Simply, because that's not who He is!

Jesus is a power under rather than a power over kind of king.

And this brings us to our second point.

The Government of the King

Kings reveal their characters by their methods of governing, and Jesus is no exception.

The prophet Isaiah foretold the birth of Christ and gave insight to the type of government He would seek to establish. Notice Isaiah 9:6-7:

> For unto us a Child is born, unto us a Son is given; and the government will be upon His shoulder. And His name will be called Wonderful, Counselor, Mighty God, Everlasting Father, Prince of Peace. Of the increase of His government and peace there will be no end, Upon the throne of David and over His kingdom, To order it and establish it with judgment and justice From that time forward, even forever. The zeal of the Lord of hosts will perform this.

Three crucial observations are in order:

1. Jesus did indeed come to our world to establish a government, and He has taken it upon Himself—upon "His shoulders"—to make sure it happens.

2. The grand goal of His government is "peace." The Hebrew word here is shalom, which is one of the most amazing and meaningful words in Scripture. Shalom is the biblical word that describes a universal condition of total well-being in which all levels of life interact with perfect harmony free from all relational conflict. Shalom is established by implementing "justice." This word means relational rectitude or righteous dealings. It is this state of affairs—shalom established though relational justice—that defines the governmental structure of Jesus.

3. His government will "increase" and have "no end." In other words, the principles upon which He operates are eternal in nature. All other methods of governing implode under the weight of injustice and oppression. The kingdom of shalom that Jesus is establishing will flourish forever because in it there is no relational violation and therefore no want. It is the only eternally sustainable system.

Now then, in practical terms, what does this type of government look like in action?

Well, we don't need to guess because Jesus came to model it for us.

The centerpiece of His teachings was that power is merely an illusion of greatness, that the truly elevated persons are those who willingly choose the humble position of ministering to the needs of others above their own. In Matthew 20:25-26, He explained the core principle of His kingdom:

> You know that the rulers of the Gentiles lord it over them, and those who are great exercise authority over them. Yet it shall not be so among you; but whoever desires to become great among you, let him be your servant.

Again, in Matthew 23:11-12, He said:

> He who is greatest among you shall be your servant. And whoever exalts himself will be humbled, and he who humbles himself will be exalted.

Jesus here taught what we might call an upside-down governmental structure. His kingdom operates as a bottom-up rather than top-down system. Greatness is defined as humility and service and love trumps all power. Love, in fact, is the most powerful power of all.

But Jesus was not dictating down to us how we ought to be as though He, as God, were the one to be served. No! He demonstrated that He, as the greatest of all, is the humblest servant of all. Said another way, He manifested His high position as king by occupying the low position of servant. Notice John 13:

> Now before the Feast of the Passover, when Jesus knew that His hour had come that He should depart from this world to the Father, having loved His own who were in the world, He loved them to the end.
>
> And supper being ended, the devil having already put it into the heart of Judas Iscariot, Simon's son, to betray Him, [3] Jesus, knowing that the Father had given all things into His hands, and that He had come from God and was going to God, rose from supper and laid aside His garments, took a towel and girded Himself. After that, He poured water into a basin and began to wash the disciples' feet, and to wipe them with the towel with which He was girded. Then He came to Simon Peter. And Peter said to Him, "Lord, are You washing my feet?"
>
> Jesus answered and said to him, "What I am doing you do not understand now, but you will know after this."
>
> Peter said to Him, "You shall never wash my feet!"
>
> Jesus answered him, "If I do not wash you, you have no part with Me."
>
> Simon Peter said to Him, "Lord, not my feet only, but also my hands and my head!"
>
> Jesus said to him, "He who is bathed needs only to wash his feet, but is completely

clean; and you are clean, but not all of you." For He knew who would betray Him; therefore He said, "You are not all clean."

So when He had washed their feet, taken His garments, and sat down again, He said to them, "Do you know what I have done to you? You call Me Teacher and Lord, and you say well, for so I am. If I then, your Lord and Teacher, have washed your feet, you also ought to wash one another's feet. For I have given you an example, that you should do as I have done to you. Most assuredly, I say to you, a servant is not greater than his master; nor is he who is sent greater than he who sent him. [17] If you know these things, blessed are you if you do them.

In this epic act of humble service, Jesus was not playing a temporary part restricted to His life as a man on earth. Rather, when we see Jesus on His knees, wrapped with a towel, washing the dirty feet of His disciples, we see God acting in true form to His eternal Godhood. This is how God always has been, how God is, and how God will always be forevermore. As Hebrews 13:8 says:

Jesus Christ is the same yesterday, today, and forever.

Astoundingly, Jesus said that even when the great war between good and evil is over and we find ourselves living in the New Earth, the One who is our King will continue serving us. Speaking of God's eternal relation to redeemed human beings, Jesus said this:

Assuredly, I say to you that He will gird Himself and have them sit down to eat, and will come and serve them. (Luke 12:37)

Wow! What a picture! You're the one seated at the table. God's the one serving the meal.

What a King!

The Law of the King

OK, so we've looked at the Character of the King and the Government of the King. Our third and final profile point is the Law of the King.
As the One true and rightful King of the universe, God is also presented in Scripture as the Lawgiver. Look at Isaiah 33:22:

For the Lord is our Judge, The Lord is our Lawgiver,
The Lord is our King; He will save us.

What's the first thing that comes to your mind when I say the word law? Is law a positive idea or a negative one? Does it conjure up feelings of confinement or freedom?

Well, it all depends what you believe about the character and government of the Lawgiver. If, as we have seen, the character of the Lawgiver is selfless love, and the governmental structure of the Lawgiver is one in which every member of the kingdom lives to serve the needs of the others, what kind of law would you expect Him to give?

Arbitrary?

Dictatorial?

Restrictive?

Absolutely not!

The law of a king like we've been seeing must be a very good law indeed.

And this is precisely what we find in Scripture.

The first indication of God's law in Scripture is found in the account of Adam and Eve in Genesis. First, consider Genesis chapter 2, verses 15 through 17:

> Then the Lord God took the man and put him in the garden of Eden to tend and keep it. And the Lord God commanded the man, saying, "Of every tree of the garden you may freely eat; but of the tree of the knowledge of good and evil you shall not eat, for in the day that you eat of it you shall surely die.

Notice here that God establishes a vast horizon of freedom with a single restriction. Of all the trees of the garden they could freely eat except one.

But someone will say, why any restriction at all? Why did God put the forbidden tree there in the first place? Was He setting them up for failure? If the tree had not been there, they would never have had the chance to sin and our world would have been spared all its misery.

But think about it: if there had been no forbidden tree, there would have been no freedom. God gave them freedom because freedom is the premise of love. Without freedom, love cannot exist. So the forbidden tree was a kind of voting booth, a place human beings could go if they wanted to break their relationship of love with their Maker. It was God's way of giving them an open door, allowing them the freedom to walk away from Him. The only alternative would have been for God to place them in a situation in which disobedience was impossible, in which case love would have been impossible. They would have been mere slaves.

So we see here, at the very genesis of the human race, that God has one law by which He governs: the law of love. And we see, as well, that this love is inseparable from the liberty we possess as free relational agents.

From this conceptual foundation, Scripture proceeds to consistently define God's law in terms of love and liberty.

Read the Ten Commandments, written with God's own finger on tables of stone, and this is what you'll discover: God's law is a comprehensive and concise declaration of what love looks like in action. The first four commandments define what love looks like in relation to God. Commandments five through ten define what love looks like toward our fellow human beings. Ingeniously, the law of God addresses all our relationships:

Commandments one through four define our relationship with God,

Five with our family,

Six through nine with others,

And ten to material stuff.

This is God's prescription for happiness: God first, family second, others next, and stuff last of all. Yet society tells us that happiness is the exact reverse of this: stuff first, others second, family next, and God last, if at all.

Imagine a world in which every person is totally content with what they have and has no desire to possess what anybody else has; a world in which nobody ever tells a lie about anybody else; a world in which every husband and wife are completely in love with one another and stay faithful; a world in which there is no hatred, violence, war, or killing; a world in which all children live with honor toward their parents and the parents are worthy of that honor; and a world in which the one and only true God, the Creator of the universe, is loved and worshipped for the good God that He is. Imagine that world, and you have imagined a world in which the Ten Commandments are the relational law by which all human beings live.

This is why Jesus summarized the Ten Commandments with the single word love—love moving vertically toward God and love moving horizontally toward our fellow human beings. In Matthew 22, a group of "law-keeping" Pharisees came to Jesus with a reductionistic question.

> Teacher, which is the great commandment in the law? (v. 36)

These guys, with their narrow legalism, thought the law could be reduced to a hierarchical list of rules that could be ticked off one by one. The answer Jesus gave indicated that the law of God is an irreducible whole, all of the Ten expressing one essential, integrated reality of other-centered love. Notice verses 37-40:

> Jesus said to him, "'You shall love the Lord your God with all your heart, with all your soul, and with all your mind.' This is the first and great commandment. And the second is like it: 'You shall love your neighbor as yourself.' On these two commandments hang all the Law and the Prophets.

The law of God is not a list of arbitrary behavioral rules, but rather the embodiment of a single relational principle, and that principle is love. This is why James could say:

> Whoever shall keep the whole Law, and yet stumble in one point, he is guilty of all. (James 2:10)

To think that you can arrange the Ten Commandments from greatest in importance to least, and then feel good about obeying one or two or even nine of them, is to completely misunderstand the intent of the law. To violate one is to violate the underlying spirit of them all.

The apostle Paul gets to the heart of what God's law is all about in Romans 13:10:

> Love does no harm to a neighbor; therefore love is the fulfillment of the Law.

Notice here that Paul defines the law as living in such a way as to do no harm to others. This is astounding if you think about it. The only things God forbids are those things that cause harm to us and to others.

Now then, once we understand that the law of God is a transcript of His character of self-giving love, the popular notion that God's law was abolished or in any way negated by Christ is seen to be ludicrous and logically indefensible. The law of God could no more be abolished than God Himself. To negate the law would be to negate love as the essence of God's character and the standard of His kingdom.

There is a monumental problem, however, when it comes to the law of God: all of us have lived outside of the parameters of the love it requires; all of us have lived in relational violation of God and others; and all of us are bankrupt of the moral power to bring our lives into harmony with God's law of love. And this is why we need a Savior.

The law of God describes what love looks like in action. Jesus came to live out God's law of love, not to eliminate it. His death on the cross magnified and sustained God's law. If the law of God could have been done away with, the death of Jesus would have been unnecessary, for it is the law that defines the problem of sin for which Jesus died to save us. So then, it logically follows that the salvation Jesus brings to us necessarily brings us back into harmony with God's law.

In Romans 8:3-4 Paul explicitly states this very thing. Notice verses 2-4:

> For the law of the Spirit of life in Christ Jesus has made me free from the law of sin and death. For what the law could not do in that it was weak through the flesh, God did by sending His own Son in the likeness of sinful flesh, on account of sin: He condemned sin in the flesh, that the righteous requirement of the law might be fulfilled in us who do not walk according to the flesh but according to the Spirit.

So Paul taught that the salvation of Christ involves "the righteousness of the Law" being "fulfilled in us." That doesn't at all sound like the law is abolished. Rather, note Paul's words, "fulfilled in us." Here Paul is pointing to what the Bible calls "the New Covenant." What is the New Covenant? It is the work of Jesus in writing His law of love in our hearts. Paul says it like this in Hebrews 10:16-17:

> This is the covenant that I will make with them after those days, says the Lord: I will put My laws into their hearts, and in their minds I will write them," then He adds, "Their sins and their lawless deeds I will remember no more.

Paul teaches us that the free grace of God by which He saves us brings about in us a quality of obedience to the law that springs forth from within. The law of God is not intended to be an externally imposed code of behavioral restrictions, but rather an internally realized law of liberty and love. James calls it "the perfect Law of liberty (James 1:25).

And Jesus, in one simple yet profound sentence, described the essence of the New Covenant like this:

> If you love Me, keep My commandments. (John 14:15)

Love is the essence of God's law, and those who partake of His love will be found living in obedience to His law.

The law of the King reveals the character of the King. It is a law of love and liberty:

1. Law that only forbids those deeds that cause hurt and harm to others,

2. and a law that expands our freedom to experience all the pleasures and wonders of life as God intended.

And so, on that note, we come full circle to our opening question:

What kind of king is Jesus?

His Character, His Government, and His Law reveal quite clearly what kind of king He is. He is self-sacrificing, humble, and good in every way imaginable.

My appeal to you and to my own heart is that we would enthrone King Jesus in our very hearts, that we recognize Him as the sovereign ruler of our lives. When we make that choice, we will discover that His only desire is to set us free to live eternally in His love.

If that is your desire, as I pray I invite you to raise your hand as a signal to heaven that you have decided to follow this One who is alone worthy to be King.

PRESENTER, PLEASE SHARE WITH YOUR AUDIENCE THAT THIS IS A SAFE ZONE.
It's a safe place to be themselves. • Everyone has the right to their own opinion. There are no dumb questions. • All comments are encouraged and respected.

Discussion Questions

1. What was your reaction to the story of King Umberto? Did your reaction change when you learned of his expansionist policies and acceptance of killing his own subjects to get his way?

2. Do you think it's always true that power corrupts, and absolute power corrupts absolutely? Can you give personal examples?

3. What do you think is meant by "anti-king"?

4. Some young men once decided the story of the incarnation of God into human flesh was completely illogical, so they chose not to believe it. A friend of one of them said, "Well, of course it's illogical—that's the whole point!" What do you think the friend meant, and what might you have said if you were part of this conversation?

5. What is your favorite thing about Jesus' character? Do you know Him personally enough to have personal examples besides Bible stories? Do you want to?

6. What has been your past opinion about the government and law of God? Has this message changed that opinion at all?

7. What would it take for you to decide to live fully in Jesus' "anti-kingdom"?

THE MAKER

THE COMMUNICATOR

THE KING

THE SAVIOR

THE SPIRIT

THE GREAT GIVER

THE HEALER

THE SACRIFICE

THE NEW MAN

THE MESSENGER

THE BRIDEGROOM

THE BODY

04. THE SAVIOR

the fall and the nature of sin

BIBLE TEXT: And I will put enmity between you and the woman, and between your seed and her seed; He shall bruise our head, and you shall bruise His heel. (Genesis 3:15)

PRESENTER'S NOTE:
- Read. Read. Read.
- Let this message soak into your mind.
- Take the time to make it your own.

Review all the discussion questions early.

the SAVIOR synopsis

Throughout history, the human race has told stories of superheroes. We seem to instinctively know we need one. The first "villain" comes into the Creation story. The devil, speaking through the serpent, lies about reality in a way that convinces the first humans to believe him. In the shame, fear, instinct to cover and hide, and blaming that results lies the seed of ongoing *internal* darkness for the whole race. There is only one true Superhero who can save us completely. Jesus, ("anti-warrior" as He is "anti-king") does not show up in a flash of muscle and light to do away with the bad guy. Instead, He comes *into* humanity as a fragile child, brings God's Word and God's Light, lives and dies as one of us—then raises us up with Him!

The Savior

We live in a world obsessed with superheroes:

- Batman
- Ironman
- Superman
- Spiderman

That's the short list.

The human imagination is hyperactive in its quest for a savior. We are possessed with a nagging sense that we are in danger and need to be rescued. And so we tell ourselves the same story over and over again: evil is out to get us and a hero comes to save us.

There is both truth and fiction in our common superhero myth. The truth is that we are in need of a savior. It is a gross fiction, however, that we need a savior who will save us from mere physical danger by means of physical violence.

The evil that poses the real threat to us is of a spiritual nature, and the savior we really need is *The One* who can liberate us from the dark realities that reside within us.

We find the real story beginning in Genesis 3, starting with verse one:

> Now the serpent was more cunning than any beast of the field which the Lord God had made. And he said to the woman, "Has God indeed said, 'You shall not eat of every tree of the garden'?"

The immediate backstory reveals that the first man and the first woman, Adam and Eve, have recently been created. Their pristine existence is characterized by three main features brought to view in Genesis 1 and 2:

1. They bear the image of God in their mental, emotional, and moral make-up, which is to say they possess freewill and the capacity for love.

2. They have genuine and open fellowship with their Maker.

3. They have a relationship with one another in which they are naked and not ashamed. They have no sense of shame because all they know is self-giving love for one another.

It is into this perfect relational environment that an enemy arrives.

The serpent was obviously one of the beautiful creatures God had made because it is here brought to view before the fall of humanity. But it is not the serpent itself that was speaking to the woman, but rather a fallen angel called Satan who once bore the name Lucifer. Satan is using the serpent as a medium of communication. This becomes clear as the story unfolds. When we come to the New Testament, we encounter Satan described with language that directly identifies him as the very same serpent of Genesis 3. Revelation 12:7-9, for example, speaks of the original war that resulted in Lucifer's expulsion from heaven:

> And war broke out in heaven: Michael and his angels fought with the dragon; and the dragon and his angels fought, but they did not prevail, nor was a place found for them in heaven any longer. So the great dragon was cast out, that serpent of old, called the Devil and Satan, who deceives the whole world; he was cast to the earth, and his angels were cast out with him.

Now let's return to Genesis 3 to observe the temptation and fall of humankind perpetrated by the serpent. In order to rightly understand the fall of mankind, it is important to notice that Satan approached humanity with *subtlety,* with an intent to deceive. The vital questions are, then, what is the specific content of his deception and who is its target? As we will see, the account reveals that God is the target and that there are three main features of the deception.

First of all, Satan casts God's relationship to humanity as one of restriction rather than freedom:

> Has God indeed said, "You shall not eat of every tree of the garden"?

The truth is, God had presented to Adam and Eve a vast horizon of freedom with only a single restriction—and that only with their best interest at heart. Notice Genesis 2:16-17:

> Of every tree of the garden you may freely eat; but of the tree of the knowledge of good and evil you shall not eat, for in the day that you eat of it you shall surely die.

But then Satan comes along and reframes the picture with the insinuation that God is exercising an unnecessary control over them. This is a foreign concept to Eve. She has not felt controlled or restricted, and so she makes an effort to refute Satan's claim. Verses 2 and 3:

> And the woman said to the serpent, "We may eat the fruit of the trees of the garden; but of the fruit of the tree which is in the midst of the garden, God has said, 'You shall not eat it, nor shall you touch it, lest you die.'"

Eve senses that she is free, that God loves her, and that He has forbidden the one tree to protect her and Adam from harm. But then the Enemy moves from an insinuation to a blunt attack on God's very character. Verse 4:

> Then the serpent said to the woman, "You will not surely die."

Here is the second feature of the deception. The intent is obvious: *God has lied to you. You can't trust Him. You will not die. It's an idle threat intended to hold you down and control you with fear.*

It's an uncomfortable feeling when you think you're being lied to and dominated. Having aroused this feeling in Eve, Satan then strikes his final blow. Verse 5:

> For God knows that in the day you eat of it your eyes will be opened, and you will be like God, knowing good and evil.

Here's the third feature of the deception. Satan now claims to know God's underlying motive for holding them under His control: *God knows something you don't—that if you break free from this needless restriction you'll be elevated to equality with Him, and He doesn't want that. God is self-serving and does not really have your best interest at heart. He doesn't love you.*

With dark genius, Satan has constructed the perfect delusion by first conjuring up a sense of confinement and then dangling before Eve the enticing prospect of an alleged freedom. *What if it's true?* she thinks. It's a tantalizing dare, and there's only one way to know. So Eve takes the plunge. Verse 6:

> So when the woman saw that the tree was good for food, that it was pleasant to the eyes, and a tree desirable to make one wise, she took of its fruit and ate. She also gave to her husband with her, and he ate.

In this account we have before us the biblical record of the fall of mankind, and the whole thing went down on the premise of a deception regarding the kind of person that God is, that is, His *character*. The behavioral part of the problem was preceded by Satan first, creating a deep perceptual distortion in the human mind. We discern, then, that the sin problem is not merely a behavioral problem. Before the *act* of sin was committed, a false picture of God was installed in the human heart. As a result, trust was broken, which then gave way to the behavioral rebellion.

It is crucial that we understand this if we are to grasp what sin is and how the Savior saves us. The disease must be correctly diagnosed if the proper remedy is to be applied.

So what happened next? In verses 7-13 we see the direct effects of the Fall. Carefully notice every aspect of this description:

> Then the eyes of both of them were opened, and they knew that they were naked; and they sewed fig leaves together and made themselves coverings. And they heard the sound of the Lord God walking in the garden in the cool of the day, and Adam and his wife hid themselves from the presence of the Lord God among the trees of the garden. Then the Lord God called to Adam and said to him, "Where are you?" So he said, "I heard Your voice in the garden, and I was afraid because I was naked; and I hid myself." And He said, "Who told you that you were naked? Have you eaten from the tree of which I commanded you that you should not eat?" Then the man said, "The woman whom You gave to be with me, she gave me of the tree, and I ate." And the Lord God said to the woman, "What is this you have done?" The woman said, "The serpent deceived me, and I ate."

Wow, things went bad in a hurry!

What we see here is that the entire mental and emotional landscape of the human soul became severely damaged and deranged. Four vital insights are brought to view in these verses:

1. *Shame.* Adam and Eve had lost something, and they "knew" it. Their eyes were opened and "they knew that they were naked." They *were* creatures of pristine innocence, but not anymore. They had been naked all along. But before the Fall their nakedness had been described in these words: "They were both naked, the man and his wife, and were not ashamed" (2:25). So the issue after the Fall is not their nakedness, per se, but self-consciousness as a result of shame. Prior to the Fall, there was no shame in their nakedness because they were completely other-centered in their orientation. Love was the psychological basis of their consciousness. But now they had become sinners, and as a result their entire orientation shifted toward selfishness.

2. *Fear.* The shame they now felt for their sin was transposed over their newly adopted picture of God, creating a sense of apprehension toward Him. They now saw their Maker as a self-serving tyrant, which generated an unnatural fear of God. The One they had loved and trusted now appeared to present a threat to them. In their state of delusion they imagined that the guilt they felt in their hearts was the result of God's attitude toward them, that their sense of self-condemnation was a reflection of God's attitude toward them. How wrong they were!

3. *Covering.* Adam and Eve made coverings for themselves in an effort to deal with their shame. Rather than turn to God for help with an expectation of mercy, the distorted view of God they now held drove them to self-dependence. Rather than seek forgiveness for their sin, they attempted to manufacture a solution for themselves. All salvation-by-works religious systems have their origin here, in the psychological derangement of self-dependence that came upon humanity as a result of the Fall.

4. *Hiding.* In addition to manufacturing coverings for themselves, they were also now possessed of an impulse to hide from God. Again, on the premise of the lie they had believed regarding the character of God, it did not occur to them to expect compassion and acceptance from God. He was now imagined to be their enemy. So they hid. And human beings have been hiding from God ever since in a myriad of obsessions, addictions, fictions, and escapist pursuits.

5. *Blaming.* Whereas before the Fall it came natural to live for one another, now it became their natural instinct to cast blame on one another and, ultimately, upon God. And human beings have been blaming one another and God ever since that day. Blame-casting is a false survival tactic for dealing with shame. By blaming others, Adam and Eve did not have to face themselves and take responsibility for their actions.

Shame. Fear. Covering. Hiding. Blaming. What a tragic and terrible list. It is the history of humanity in five short words!

All of this was, and is, the dark aftermath of the Fall. And all of it is our inheritance as human beings in the lineage of Adam and Eve. We're all infected mentally and emotionally with the primal lie of the enemy in some form or another, to one degree or another.

We all have trust issues, especially with God.

We're all strongly inclined to selfishness and rebellion in our relationships.

We all carry secret and/or subconscious shame as a result of our sins.

We're all uncertain of God's character and therefore afraid of Him.

We all incline toward manufacturing our own salvation and find it natural to believe that God must be appeased and His favor earned by our deeds.

We all hide from one another and from God in various obsessions, addictions, false narratives, and fictitious projections of ourselves.

And we all cast blame on others and on God as a way of evading our own guilt.

We are, all in all, quite messed up, deceived, dysfunctional, and downright sinful.

But–*good news!*–that's not the end of the story, because Satan is a liar and God is nothing like the enemy has portrayed Him to be. In fact, as we are about to discover, God is love in the most beautiful sense imaginable. This being the case, God immediately set in motion a proactive plan to rescue us.

This brings us to Genesis 3:15:

> And I will put enmity between you and the woman, and between your seed and her Seed; He shall bruise your head, and you shall bruise His heel.

Here we have the first gospel promise—the promise of good news! It came in the form of a declaration of war spoken by God directly to Satan in the hearing of Adam and Eve. God has come to the defense of fallen humanity. He addresses our assailant by foretelling that a Warrior will be sent through the woman, through human lineage, to save the fallen race. *The One* and only true Savior is coming. This promised Warrior will crush the head of the Serpent and will wound His own heel in the process. In this prophecy we have the first indication in Scripture of the incarnation and sufferings of Christ. From this point forward, the various prophets of the Old Testament add layers of detail to fill out the character and mission of the coming Savior as *The One* who will fulfill this covenant promise.

You will notice that God expresses Himself here in a definite manner: "I will," He says. This is why we call Genesis 3:15 a "promise." God is here vowing Himself by the absolute certainty of a covenant pledge to do something, namely to conquer Satan on our behalf.

And how will He do it?

Well, not how we might expect. Not like Superman, Batman, or any other man-made superhero would!

Just as we discovered in our previous message that Jesus is an anti-king kind of king, we will now discover that He is an anti-warrior kind of warrior. He fights, not with weapons of force and violence, but rather with the far more formidable weapons of truth and love.

Announcing His arrival to our world, John characterized the promised Warrior as "the Word" and "the Light." Take a look at John 1:1-5:

> In the beginning was the Word, and the Word was with God, and the Word was God. He was in the beginning with God. All things were made through Him, and without Him nothing was made that was made. In Him was life, and the life was the light of men. And the light shines in the darkness, and the darkness did not comprehend it [overcome it, NIV].

Jesus comes to "overcome" the "darkness" and save fallen humanity as *Word* and *Light*. Words carry information and light enables and sharpens vision. Both operate as mediums of clarity. Don't miss that! I'll say it again: both bring clarity!

So, Jesus embarks upon our rescue by the conveyance of knowledge and illumination. This makes such sense when we remember that the fall of mankind was achieved by the conveyance of misinformation and darkness regarding the character of God. Now Jesus comes as the true Word and the true Light to deal with the darkness, and the darkness has no chance of overcoming the light He emits.

So what precisely is the Word that Jesus has for us and the Light He shines upon us?

Skip down to verse 14:

> And the Word became flesh and dwelt among us, and we beheld His glory, the glory as of the only begotten of the Father, full of grace and truth.

John wants us to understand that Jesus came into our benighted world so we could "behold" something, *see* something. See what, exactly? The text says, "His glory," which is the glory of the Father as well. The word here translated "glory" is *doxa* in the Greek. It simply means an "opinion" or "estimate" or "view" of a person. In the New Testament it "always refers to a good opinion concerning one, resulting in praise, honor, and glory" (*Strong* Greek Concordance). Therefore, *doxa* is translated as "glory" in the sense that God is glorified when we have a correct estimate or view of what manner of person He really is. Jesus came to our world to communicate (as the Word) and reveal (as the Light) an accurate opinion, estimate, and view of God's character. This intent is made clear in verse 18:

> No one has seen God at any time. The only begotten Son, who is in the bosom of the Father, He has declared Him.

Jesus came to "declare" the Father, being qualified by the fact that He came from the "bosom" of the Father, or as the New International Version says, from "closest relationship with the Father." This is the Promised One. The Savior. The Hero we really need. He has come to speak the Word of truth concerning the character of God. Indeed, He *is* the Word of truth.

And what will the effect of His ministry be?

In verse 29, when John the Baptist sees Jesus, he announces: "Behold! The Lamb of God who takes away the sin of the world!"

Jesus has come to deal with the sin problem!

Just like that first promise in Eden had announced and foretold!

And how will He do it?

John's Gospel opens by informing us that Jesus is the Word and the Light who has come to reveal the true character of God, and now we see that He is also the Lamb. The symbolism of the lamb invokes the sacrificial ceremonies of the Old Testament, beginning in Eden when God made "coverings" for Adam and Eve from the skin of the first animal sacrifice, then developed in the covenant sacrifice God instituted with Abraham in Genesis 15, then developed with yet greater detail in the sanctuary constructed by Moses in the wilderness. In each case, the sacrifices pointed to the self-sacrifice of God in the coming Messiah.

Paul would later interpret the sacrifice of Christ as the means by which God "demonstrated His own love for us, in that while we were still sinners Christ died for us" (Romans 5:8).

Here we see that God's love was "demonstrated" in the concrete historic fact that "Christ died for us." Rather than abandoning us to our rightful demise, He put Himself in our place as our substitute. The prophet Isaiah foretold the substitutionary death of Christ with language horrific and beautiful. Listen with your whole heart to every line:

> All we like sheep have gone astray; We have turned, every one, to his own way; And the Lord has laid on Him the iniquity of us all.
>
> He was oppressed and He was afflicted, Yet He opened not His mouth; He was led as a lamb to the slaughter, And as a sheep before its shearers is silent, So He opened not His mouth. He was taken from prison and from judgment, And who will declare His generation? For He was cut off from the land of the living; For the transgressions of My people He was stricken. And they made His grave with the wicked—But with the rich at His death, Because He had done no violence, Nor was any deceit in His mouth.
>
> Yet it pleased the Lord to bruise Him; He has put Him to grief. When You make His soul an offering for sin, He shall see His seed, He shall prolong His days, And the pleasure of the Lord shall prosper in His hand. He shall see the labor of His soul,

and be satisfied. By His knowledge My righteous Servant shall justify many, For He shall bear their iniquities.

Therefore I will divide Him a portion with the great, And He shall divide the spoil with the strong, Because He poured out His soul unto death, And He was numbered with the transgressors, And He bore the sin of many, And made intercession for the transgressors. (Isaiah 53:6-12)

Did you catch all of that? We're all sinners, the prophet says. Due to our sins, we each bear a load of guilt. We stand guilty before God and before our own conscience. But rather than leave us to bear our shame and suffer its terrible consequences ourselves, "the Lord has laid on him the iniquity of us all." As a voluntary act of self-sacrificing love, Jesus was "led as a lamb to the slaughter." Though perfectly innocent, He was judged as "wicked," "numbered with the transgressors," and then "poured out his soul unto death" on our behalf.

In 2 Corinthians 5:21, Paul beautifully summarizes Isaiah's prophecy in a single sentence:

For He made Him who knew no sin to be sin for us, that we might become the righteousness of God in Him.

And why did He do this?

For the simple and yet profound reason that He literally loves you more than His own life. In Hebrews 9:26, we read this astounding insight:

He has appeared to put away sin by the sacrifice of Himself.

Wow! Self-sacrificing love was the means and mechanism of our salvation.

And so we see that the *revelatory* aspect of God's plan to save and this *substitutionary* aspect dovetail to compose one achievement of supreme love for a lost humanity.

Moving forward from John 1, we see a pattern of purpose that builds to a climax at the cross where Jesus dies as the sacrificial Lamb of God. Let's trace the pattern.

When the first miracle of Jesus is performed, John says:

This beginning of signs Jesus did in Cana of Galilee, and manifested His glory; and His disciples believed in Him. (John 2:11)

Notice John's explicit point: In this first miracle of hospitable kindness, Jesus was manifesting the "glory," the *doxa*, of His character. This of course loops back to chapter 1, verse 14, in which John announces that the Word became flesh and lived among us so that we could behold the glory of the Father in Him.

In Chapter 3:16-17 Jesus marries the revelation of the Father's love with His up-and-coming sacrifice on the cross:

> And as Moses lifted up the serpent in the wilderness, even so must the Son of Man be lifted up, that whoever believes in Him should not perish but have eternal life. For God so loved the world that He gave His only begotten Son, that whoever believes in Him should not perish but have everlasting life. For God did not send His Son into the world to condemn the world, but that the world through Him might be saved.

At least three crucial points stand out here:

First: We see that the sacrifice of Jesus was made because God loves us, not in order to induce God to love us. This flies in the face of every other notion of sacrifice throughout history in all religions. The common conception, as an outgrowth of Satan's original lie in Eden, is that human beings must suffer and sacrifice in order to appease God and earn His love. Here Jesus teaches the opposite: God already loves us, and because of His love He voluntarily sacrifices Himself on our behalf.

Second: Jesus explains that God's love is defined by the fact that He does not condemn us. Condemnation is Satan's disposition, and he would like for us to believe that it is God's disposition. Jesus demonstrated that God stands toward us with an attitude of pardoning love.

Third: Jesus here teaches that His self-sacrificing death on the cross is the means by which God saves us.

Now come to John chapter 12:23-32 and notice the language carefully:

> But Jesus answered them, saying, "The hour has come that the Son of Man should be glorified. Most assuredly, I say to you, unless a grain of wheat falls into the ground and dies, it remains alone; but if it dies, it produces much grain. He who loves his life will lose it, and he who hates his life in this world will keep it for eternal life. If anyone serves Me, let him follow Me; and where I am, there My servant will be also. If anyone serves Me, him My Father will honor. "Now My soul is troubled, and what shall I say? 'Father, save Me from this hour'? But for this purpose I came to this hour. Father, glorify Your name." Then a voice came from heaven, saying, "I have both glorified it and will glorify it again." Therefore the people who stood

by and heard it said that it had thundered. Others said, "An angel has spoken to Him." Jesus answered and said, "This voice did not come because of Me, but for your sake. Now is the judgment of this world; now the ruler of this world will be cast out. And I, if I am lifted up from the earth, will draw all peoples to Myself." [33] This He said, signifying by what death He would die.

Here Jesus states the "purpose" of His sacrificial death on the cross: to manifest His glory and the glory of His Father; that is, to reveal the character of God. And this will produce two grand and astounding achievements:

1. Satan will be cast out. His lies regarding the character of God will be drained of their credibility.

2. All people will be drawn to God through Christ as His death on the cross reveals that, indeed, God is love.

The death of Jesus on the cross is the complete fulfillment of the promise of Genesis 3:15. Not with coercion and violence, but with truth in love, Jesus crushed the head of the serpent under His heel. He counteracted the lie Satan had told regarding the character of God and died as the sacrificial Lamb.

And so it was, in Jesus Christ, that every aspect of the sin problem was resolved:

1. The cross reveals God's free forgiveness for our sins, thus lifting our *shame* and restoring our innocence before Him.

2. The cross relieves our illegitimate *fear* of God by repainting His true character upon our hearts.

3. The cross provides the true *covering* we need—the "love" of God that effectually "covers a multitude of sins" (1 Peter 4:8).

4. The cross draws us to God out of our *hiding* places—our obsessions, addictions, and every self-destructive behavior—into the light of His reassuring love.

5. And the cross gives us the moral courage to cease *blaming* others and take responsibility for our sins through confession and repentance.

All of our world's hero myths tell the common story of danger and deliverance, but all of them fall short of our real need. We know we're in trouble, but ultimately we don't need a hero to save us from mere physical danger. We need a Savior to deliver us from the deceptions of Satan that distort our perceptions of God, from the sins we have committed in rebellion against God, and from the shame those sins have imposed upon our conscience.

Jesus is that Savior. He is *The One* we so desperately need.

In the beautiful light that streams from the cross of Christ, I invite you to turn to Him, to give your heart to Him, to place your sins upon Him and receive the forgiveness of God through Him, to receive Him as your personal Savior.

No more shame!

No more fear!

No more vain efforts to cover your sins!

No more hiding in whatever obsessions or addictions that bind you!

No more blaming others!

Come to the cross. Look by faith upon The One hanging there, burying your sin and guilt. Believe with your heart and confess with your mouth that Jesus is the Savior you need.

If that is your desire, please slip to your knees with me as we pray, and if you would like to make this prayer your own, simply say amen after me.

PRESENTER, PLEASE SHARE WITH YOUR AUDIENCE THAT THIS IS A SAFE ZONE.
It's a safe place to be themselves. • Everyone has the right to their own opinion.
There are no dumb questions. • All comments are encouraged and respected.

Discussion Questions

1. Who is your favorite imaginary superhero? Why?

2. How does this superhero measure up when compared with Jesus?

3. What do you need to be rescued from?

4. What is your reaction to the story of the serpent in the garden?

5. Looking at Genesis 3 in a Bible, list some of the things the humans immediately lost.

6. How have shame, fear, covering/hiding, and blame been active in your life?

7. What have you tried to get free of those painful things? Has it worked?

8. What does it mean to you to think of Jesus taking on that shame, fear, and blame for you, and bringing you tenderly out of hiding and into His light?

STEPS TO
discipleship

STEPS TO discipleship

STEPS TO
discipleship

Produced by
General Conference
Youth Ministries Department

THE POWER OF ONE

The perfect gift to help young adults discover a faith of THEIR OWN!

A SEVEN WEEK JOURNEY TO AUTHENTIC DISCIPLESHIP

VISIT WWW.GCYOUTHMINISTRIES.ORG AND DOWNLOAD YOUR FREE COPY TODAY.

THE MAKER

THE COMMUNICATOR

THE KING

THE SAVIOR

THE SPIRIT

THE GREAT GIVER

THE HEALER

THE SACRIFICE

THE NEW MAN

THE MESSENGER

THE BRIDEGROOM

THE BODY

05. THE SPIRIT
the work of the holy spirit

BIBLE TEXT: If you love Me, keep My commandments. And I will pray the Father, and He will give you another Helper, that He may abide with you forever—the Spirit of truth, whom the world cannot receive, because it neither sees Him nor knows Him; but you know Him, for He dwells with you and will be in you. I will not leave you orphans; I will come to you. (John 14:15-18)

the SPIRIT synopsis

This message looks at the Holy Spirit from three perspectives: the Coming of the Spirit, the Confirmation of the Spirit, and the Conflict of the Spirit. Jesus' promises of the Holy Spirit's coming are recorded especially in John, through whom we learn that the Spirit is a helper, lives in us, testifies of Jesus, will teach us "all things," and will be of great advantage to us. Acts records the Spirit's incredible empowerment of the infant church. What Jesus had planted by His life, death, and resurrection, the Spirit was now watering and bringing to fruition and harvest in His followers. When we let Him in, the Spirit shows up and causes conflict, both with the world and with one's inner self. But through that conflict, if we stick with Him and never give up, we will find immeasurable peace and victory.

The Spirit

Let's start with a simple word association exercise. If I say, "school," what images come to your mind? Maybe books, children, a school bus, paper, pens and pencils, and a teacher? You get the idea. Let's try a couple more—and remember—think of the *images* that come to mind. How about "wedding"? And "food"?

Now that you're warmed up, let me give you what may be a hard one: "spirit." Hmmm. That's a tougher one, isn't it? What, after all, does a *spirit* look like? Maybe something like vapor or smoke came to your mind. Maybe it was something else entirely. It's more difficult because, unlike school, wedding, food, or other more concrete words, "spirit" doesn't, for most of us, create an immediate visual image that comes to mind.

What, really, is a spirit?

And what did it mean when Jesus said, "God is spirit" (John 4:24)?

These are important questions that demand our thoughtful attention. In our last presentation we learned of the One who is the Savior, Jesus Christ. We learned of rescue from the sin problem and from death, shame, fear, self-dependence, hiding, and blaming. We learned of Satan's casting out and of the vindication of God's character of love. We learned that when we believe, God declares us righteous and clean based on the Savior's faithfulness and righteousness! Jesus Christ, truly, is the Savior!

But what happens next? This is where the biblical truth of the Spirit comes in. And what a beautiful, powerful, and life-changing truth it is. We'll look at the Holy Spirit from three perspectives—through three lenses. They are:

1. The Coming of the Spirit

2. The Confirmation of the Spirit

3. The Conflict of the Spirit

1. The Coming of the Spirit

In our opening lesson, "The Maker," you'll recall that we learned that Scripture identifies God as three persons who collectively compose one God: God the Father, God the Son, and God the Holy Spirit; these three live eternally in self-giving love for one another. And what a profoundly beautiful picture of God this is. John captured the essence of this truth in the simple but infinitely deep phrase: "God is love" (1 John 4:8).

John says that God is more than merely *loving*, He is love in His essential nature and character. So love is more than merely something God *does*, it's something that He *is*.

God's love is the very basis and reason of Creation. It is also the very basis for our re-creation into what Paul called "a new creation" (2 Corinthians 5:17). Just as "the Spirit of God was hovering over the face of the waters" ready to play an active role in Creation in Genesis 1:2, the Spirit hovers over those who believe—His new creation. But, as we'll learn in this lesson, the Spirit does not merely surround us, He also dwells *in* us!

Jesus often spoke of His coming death and resurrection, but the disciples were slow to comprehend and believe His words. And with good reason, since no first-century Jew was anticipating a crucified and dead Messiah! Quite the opposite, they had, for more than a thousand years, been anticipating and awaiting a deliverer, one who would free them from their hated enemies and oppressors. They were looking for a David-like warrior, not a humble healer and parable-teller from no-name Nazareth.

And yet Jesus' influence was gaining a certain kind of grassroots momentum that the religious leaders and establishment could neither understand nor stop. Jesus' picture of God's character and kingdom was truly revolutionary; it threatened to upend the religious hierarchy and establishment of His day. Jesus was not blind to the implications of His preaching, teaching, and healing, and He understood fully well that it would excite suspicion, fear, and hatred from many.

Jesus, though, pressed on, preaching, teaching, healing, loving, and inviting. He was, literally, on a mission, and nothing and no one was going to stop Him, try though they might.

> Now while they were staying in Galilee, Jesus said to them, 'The Son of Man is about to be betrayed into the hands of men, and they will kill Him, and the third day He will be raised up.' And they were exceedingly sorrowful. (Matthew 17:22, 23)

Jesus' predictions came to pass exactly as He had said:

> Now it came to pass, when Jesus had finished all these sayings, that He said to His disciples, "You know that after two days is the Passover, and the Son of Man will be delivered up to be crucified." Then the chief priests, the scribes, and the elders of the people assembled at the palace of the high priest, who was called Caiaphas, and plotted to take Jesus by trickery and kill Him. (Matthew 26:1-4)

But Jesus knew that apparent defeat would bring actual victory, for He had two "secret weapons": His resurrection and the Spirit!

Jesus repeatedly spoke of both to His followers and disciples, but their misconceptions about the Messiah and His mission prevented them from grasping their significance. John, in particular, records some of Jesus' plainest announcements about the coming of the Spirit:

> If you love Me, keep My commandments. And I will pray the Father, and He will give you another Helper, that He may abide with you forever—the Spirit of truth, whom the world cannot receive, because it neither sees Him nor knows Him; but you know Him, for He dwells with you and will be in you. I will not leave you orphans; I will come to you. (John 14:15-18)

> These things I have spoken to you while being present with you. But the Helper, the Holy Spirit, whom the Father will send in My name, He will teach you all things, and bring to your remembrance all things that I said to you. (John 14:25, 46)

> But when the Helper comes, whom I shall send to you from the Father, the Spirit of truth who proceeds from the Father, He will testify of Me. And you also will bear witness, because you have been with Me from the beginning. (John 15:26, 27)

> But because I have said these things to you, sorrow has filled your heart. Nevertheless I tell you the truth. It is to your advantage that I go away; for if I do not go away, the Helper will not come to you; but if I depart, I will send Him to you. And when He has come, He will convict the world of sin, and of righteousness, and of judgment. (John 16:6-8)

Let's note several things from these passages:

1. The Holy Spirit is called the Helper, which means, of course, that He would be a great help to believers following Jesus' return to His Father in heaven.

2. Jesus said the Holy Spirit would be "in you"! That is, He would do what even Jesus Himself was not able to do: live *inside* of His followers.

3. The Holy Spirit will teach you "all things" and bring Jesus' life and teachings to the remembrance of His followers.

4. The Holy Spirit will come from both the Father and Jesus and He will testify, not of Himself, but of Jesus.

5. Something about Jesus' leaving and the Spirit's coming would be to the disciples' "advantage" because the Spirit would carry on a world-encompassing work.

Sure enough, following Jesus' resurrection, He spoke to His disciples about the promise of the Spirit. Luke records this promise in the opening of the book of Acts:

> And being assembled together with them, He commanded them not to depart from Jerusalem, but to wait for the Promise of the Father, 'which,' He said, 'you have heard from Me; for John truly baptized with water, but you shall be baptized with the Holy Spirit not many days from now'. (Acts 1:4, 5)

He continued,
> But you shall receive power when the Holy Spirit has come upon you; and you shall be witnesses to Me in Jerusalem, and in all Judea and Samaria, and to the end of the earth. (Acts 1:8)

Jesus had lived, died, and rose again, and was now preparing to return to His Father's side in heaven. But He would not leave His disciples alone and confused; He would not, He said, leave them as "orphans." He would send them help—no wonder the Spirit would be called the Helper!

2. The Confirmation of the Holy Spirit

Jesus was not kidding or exaggerating about the Holy Spirit being powerful! The disciples found this out fifty days after Jesus' crucifixion on what was called the Day of Pentecost. Pentecost, appropriately enough, means fiftieth day, as this Jewish festival was held on the fiftieth day after the second day of Passover.

There is enormous significance to all of this! For the Jew, the Passover hearkened all the way back, more than a thousand years, to the time of Moses and the Exodus from

Egypt. Pharaoh had been unwilling to let the Jewish slaves go free, so God had sent nine successive plagues to persuade him. Still he refused.

The tenth plague, though, would loosen his grip, and what a terrible plague it was: the death of the firstborn, including Pharaoh's own son. But Moses had instructed the Jews what to do as the plague of judgment approached. They were to take a lamb into their house and prepare unleavened bread. On the day of the plague the lamb was to be slain and eaten with the unleavened bread, and the blood of the lamb was to be placed on the doorway of each Jewish dwelling. When the destroying plague came that night, the Jewish homes were passed-over because of the blood of the lamb, thus the name Passover. Not one of the Jewish firstborn died. You can read all about this in the first twelve chapters of the book of Exodus.

That lamb represented Jesus and His death for us! A death that saves us from the destroying plague of death.

The Passover was a continual reminder to the Jews of the faithfulness and mercy of God and of the saving death of the Lamb. Year after year and generation after generation, it was celebrated.

Fifty days after Passover was Pentecost, also called the Feast of Weeks since there were seven weeks between the two. Seven times seven is forty-nine, so the next day would be, you guessed it, the fiftieth! On that day, in the ancient Jewish festival, the priest would wave a special offering of the "first fruits" before God. It was a powerful symbol of the coming harvest that was made available by the deliverance of Passover fifty days before.

So something powerful and special would happen on Pentecost—something that would foreshadow a great harvest and celebration.

And that's exactly what happened!

According to Luke's account in Acts 2, "about three thousand" people were baptized into faith in Jesus Christ (verse 41). The harvest was here! Not a harvest of grain, but of people, saved by their belief and trust in the Messiah!

Peter and the others preached with the supernatural enabling of the Holy Spirit. Jesus Christ and His death—His Passover!—and resurrection were preached with power and conviction. Jesus' promise from John 12:32 was coming to pass right before the disciples' amazed eyes:

> And I, if I am lifted up from the earth, will draw all peoples to Myself.

As Peter was bringing his sermon to a close, he uttered these amazing words regarding Jesus death and resurrection:

> This Jesus God has raised up, of which we are all witnesses. Therefore being exalted to the right hand of God, and having received from the Father the promise of the Holy Spirit, He poured out this which you now see and hear. (Acts 2:32, 33)

The Spirit's confirmation was seen all over the ministry and lives of Jesus' followers. What Jesus had planted by His life, death, and resurrection, the Spirit was now watering and bringing to fruition and harvest. Again, Jesus had foretold it:

> Most assuredly, I say to you, unless a grain of wheat falls into the ground and dies, it remains alone; but if it dies, it produces much grain. (John 12:24)

Jesus, "the grain of wheat," had literally died and gone "into the ground"—His tomb!—and now that death was producing "much grain."

Just as Matthew, Mark, Luke, and John are the books of the *acts* of Jesus Christ, Acts is the book of the *acts* of the Spirit in and through the early church. A few select passages make this clear:

> And when they had prayed, the place where they were assembled together was shaken; and they were all filled with the Holy Spirit, and they spoke the word of God with boldness. (Acts 4:31)

> Him God has exalted to His right hand to be Prince and Savior, to give repentance to Israel and forgiveness of sins. And we are His witnesses to these things, and so also is the Holy Spirit whom God has given to those who obey Him. (Acts 5:31, 32)

> Then the churches throughout all Judea, Galilee, and Samaria had peace and were edified. And walking in the fear of the Lord and in the comfort of the Holy Spirit, they were multiplied. (Acts 9:31)

The church was on the move because the Holy Spirit was on the move. Yes, there was significant opposition and danger, but the Spirit continued to do exactly what Jesus had said He would: He gave them boldness, remembrance, comfort, power, and companionship. Though He was not visible, as Jesus had been during His earthly ministry, the effects of His power, influence, and indwelling were clearly seen, just as the wind, though unseen, is clearly shown by its effects.

The work of the Spirit was extending, broadening, and making available the salvation

Jesus had secured by His life, death, and resurrection. People by the thousands were being converted and changed. Families were being healed and strengthened. Diseased and broken bodies were being restored. Churches were springing up all over. Jews and Gentiles alike were being drawn to God's love and forgiveness in Jesus Christ. Enemies of the gospel, like Saul, were being transformed into its greatest advocates and evangelists.

Great and powerful things were happening, and they were happening because people, ordinary people, were being filled and transformed by the Spirit, just as Jesus had foretold and promised. Jesus' words were unmistakable:

> Most assuredly, I say to you, he who believes in Me, the works that I do he will do also; and greater works than these he will do, because I go to My Father. (John 14:12)

Greater works? Yes, *greater* works! Greater in terms of *scope* and *reach*. Whereas Jesus was confined by His humanity in both space and time, the Spirit could be in all places He was needed *at the same time!* No wonder Jesus had said,

> Nevertheless I tell you the truth. It is to your advantage that I go away; for if I do not go away, the Helper will not come to you; but if I depart, I will send Him to you. (John 16:7)

The effects of the Holy Spirit were not seen only or even primarily in the "big" events and among the "big" crowds. The secret of the Spirit's success is in the transforming of individual lives. The Spirit does, yes, accomplish great and world-impacting things, but He does so one changed life at a time. The early church was filled with the Spirit because the individual followers of Jesus who made up the church were filled with the Spirit!

And so it is today! The work of the Spirit, though far-reaching and broad, happens one life at a time.

When a person—a person just like you—accepts the salvation that Jesus offers, then the Spirit comes into their life and confirms to them that they are a saved child of God. Consider the following passage from Paul in Romans 8:14-16:

> For as many as are led by the Spirit of God, these are sons of God. For you did not receive the spirit of bondage again to fear, but you received the Spirit of adoption by whom we cry out, "Abba, Father." The Spirit Himself bears witness with our spirit that we are children of God.

Paul was someone who had been saved and changed by Jesus Christ, so he knew what he was writing about. Notice that when we receive the Spirit, according to Paul, He comes into our life and cries out from inside of us, "Abba, Father." That is, the Spirit comes inside of the believer and calls out to God from *within*. And who is that call to? Abba! Father! We can now, by the Spirit's confirmation, call God our Father. And notice that last line in verse 16: "the Spirit Himself bears witness with our spirit that we are children of God." What a promise and a revelation!

The Spirit tells us in our spirits, that is, in our *hearts*, in our *innermost being*, that we are God's children, His sons and daughters. Can there be a better promise than that? I can't think of one!

Paul speaks of this confirming promise in another profoundly encouraging passage, Galatians 4:6, 7:

> And because you are sons, God has sent forth the Spirit of His Son into your hearts, crying out, 'Abba, Father!' Therefore you are no longer a slave but a son, and if a son, then an heir of God through Christ.

Let that language sink in: you are not slaves, but sons! Sons and daughters of God!

And how, according to Scripture, do we know this? Because the Spirit tells us so Himself!

Remember that Jesus said that the Spirit would "convict the world of sin, and of righteousness, and of judgment" (John 16:8). Don't miss this truth that's emerging right before our eyes. The Spirit performs two primary and complimentary works: He *convicts* and He *confirms*.

He convicts the world, that is, unbelievers, of sin—*what is wrong*, righteousness—*what is right*, and judgment—*what is coming*. This convicting work is designed to arrest the attention of the individual and direct them to their tremendous need of a Savior. The Spirit, who comforts the afflicted, also afflicts the comfortable! He presses the soul's need for a Savior heavy upon the unbelieving heart by reminding it of sin, righteousness, and judgment.

And when an unbeliever can take the heaviness of the Spirit's conviction no more and turns wholeheartedly to the Savior, then immediately the Spirit's work of confirmation takes place! Once someone places their faith in Jesus Christ, they become a son or a daughter of God—what the Bible calls a "joint heir" with Christ (Romans 8:17). This means that just as God the Father is Jesus Christ's Father, He is now the believer's Father! What a picture of family unity and love. This promise of being "joint heirs" with Jesus Christ comes immediately after the passage in Romans 8 that we just looked at. Here's the whole passage in its context:

> For as many as are led by the Spirit of God, these are sons of God. For you did not receive the spirit of bondage again to fear, but you received the Spirit of adoption by whom we cry out, "Abba, Father." The Spirit Himself bears witness with our spirit that we are children of God, and if children, then heirs—heirs of God and joint heirs with Christ, if indeed we suffer with Him, that we may also be glorified together.

So the confirmation of the Spirit's work was seen all over the early church, and the reason is that each individual member of the church had received the personal confirmation from the Spirit that God was their Father and Jesus was their Savior.

So does this mean that everything is easy from that point on? Is it all smooth sailing into the harbor now?

Not at all! And that's what we turn our attention to now in the third and final part of our lesson: The Conflict of the Spirit.

3. The Conflict of the Spirit

When someone places their faith in Jesus, as we have seen, they become a saved and rescued child of God. And yet this transformation from what *was* to what *now is* doesn't happen without a struggle. Placing one's faith in Jesus is, in many ways, not the end of conflict but its beginning! The reason is that the new believer is at odds both with the world around him/her and the world inside him/her. Let's talk about both of these.

External Conflict
The external conflict is an easy one to understand and anticipate, since this world operates largely on the principles of selfishness. Fame, appearance, power, control, manipulation, materialism, and consumerism are some the values upon which this world too often turns. Selfishness and self-centeredness are seen in nearly every area of life: politics, fashion, business, education, sports, and more. Even families and

relationships are not exempt. In so many ways, this world is all about "me"! The rest of you are just supporting actors in my life's movie; I am the star.

We may not say or think it in just this way, but the basic reality of our self-centered, me-first world cannot be denied. "The survival of the fittest" is not just an evolutionary term. It's the way our world operates.

Scripture confirms this dismal and selfish picture of the world. John writes in 1 John 2:15-17,

> Do not love the world or the things in the world. If anyone loves the world, the love of the Father is not in him. For all that is in the world—the lust of the flesh, the lust of the eyes, and the pride of life—is not of the Father but is of the world. And the world is passing away, and the lust of it; but he who does the will of God abides forever.

At the end of his letter, John reminded his readers that, "the whole world lies under the sway of the wicked one" (1John 5:19).

Jesus went so far as to repeatedly refer to Satan, the enemy, as "the ruler of this world" (John 12:31; 14:30; 16:11).

From a biblical perspective, in a very real sense this world belongs to Satan since it operates on his principles. Jesus came to take this world back, and this happens in large by the work of the Spirit in the believer's life. But it isn't easy! Once one confesses Christ and recognizes Him as the true "ruler of this world," a conflict ensues. Worldly ambitions, aspirations, entertainments, and enticements become unattractive to the follower of Jesus. This places Jesus' followers at odds with the prevailing culture and values. Conflict is inevitable.

This external conflict can take on many forms. Perhaps you are mocked and despised by friends or former friends, or you find it difficult to participate in the activities you used to find so enjoyable, and your friends or family can't understand what's "wrong" with you. Perhaps a co-worker is using lies and misrepresentations to get ahead of you in your workplace. Or maybe your teachers and professors are openly mocking your faith in God.

The conflict can be fierce and sustained, yes, but what complicates matters still further is that this conflict is not merely external, it is internal as well!

Internal Conflict

The teaching of Scripture is that our natural internal desires are at significant odds with our newly-acquired God-given desires. By nature and birth we are inclined toward selfishness; by our rebirth in Christ we are now inclined toward love and selflessness. This creates an obvious conflict. Listen to how Scripture describes this reality:

> For the flesh lusts against the Spirit, and the Spirit against the flesh; and these are contrary to one another, so that you do not do the things that you wish. (Galatians 5:17)

This whole passage in Galatians 5 is well worth your time and thoughtful attention.

Here's another passage in which Paul describes his own internal conflict between the Spiritual nature and the worldly nature:

> For we know that the law is spiritual, but I am carnal, sold under sin. For what I am doing, I do not understand. For what I will to do, that I do not practice; but what I hate, that I do... For I know that in me (that is, in my flesh) nothing good dwells; for to will is present with me, but how to perform what is good I do not find. For the good that I will to do, I do not do; but the evil I will not to do, that I practice. Now if I do what I will not to do, it is no longer I who do it, but sin that dwells in me. (Romans 7:14, 15, 18-20)

Compared to this internal conflict between the old nature and the new nature, the external conflict can sometimes feel like a rest!

The work of the Spirit is no easy or simple work. It's the work of a lifetime! A life of conflict may not sound very attractive, but before you get discouraged and tempted to just give up, remember Jesus' promise that He would not leave us as "orphans." He knows that there will be times when the battle is particularly hard, and it is at these moments when, perhaps, He feels the farthest, that He is, in fact, the nearest. Cling to those words: "I will never leave you nor forsake you" (Hebrews 13:5).

It's when the conflict is the severest that the victories gained by the Spirit are the sweetest! And one victory will lead to another and still another. Sure, there may be failures, but do not despair. In fact, don't even *think* of despairing since Jesus Christ's forgiveness is always there to catch you. If you fall and fail, turn to Jesus and claim His mighty promise: "If we confess our sins, He is faithful and just to forgive us our sins and to cleanse us from all unrighteousness" (1 John 1:9).

If you fall and fail, be honest with God. Don't try to justify or rationalize your sin, just confess it. Tell Him that you failed and that you hate failing. Tell Him that you're sorry and that you don't want to fail Him again. Then cling to the promise of His forgiveness and get back up again. Like the old Proverb says, "For a righteous man may fall seven times, and rise again" (Proverbs 24:16).

If you fall, get back up. It's that simple.

And do you know what? Over time, right before your eyes, you will become more and more reliant on the Spirit, and where once there was failure, you will find victory. You may feel weak and helpless. No problem. Those are just the kinds of people that Jesus came to save! In fact, according to Scripture, when you feel the weakest it's then that you are actually at your strongest. Strange but true. "My grace is sufficient for you, for My strength is made perfect in weakness" (2 Corinthians 12:9).

The strength that gains the victory is not your strength, but the Spirit's!

And in a strange way, the key to victory in this conflict, both external and internal, comes when we learn to surrender and rely on the Spirit's power. He is, after all, God, and as such has much more power and strength than you or me.

The conflict may be difficult, but two things are certain: the forgiveness and acceptance of Jesus Christ through it all and the Spirit's eventual victory over every last bit of selfishness. By His grace, we can learn to live lives of genuine love and godliness.

Believe it! Accept it! Live it!

You are not an orphan, but a child of God the King, confirmed by the Spirit!

PRESENTER, PLEASE SHARE WITH YOUR AUDIENCE THAT THIS IS A SAFE ZONE.
It's a safe place to be themselves. • Everyone has the right to their own opinion.
There are no dumb questions. • All comments are encouraged and respected.

Discussion Questions

1. In your small group, discuss your first responses to what visual image, if any, came to mind for the word "spirit."

2. In what ways has the Spirit of God shown Himself in your life? In what ways would you like Him to?

3. In what ways has the Spirit confirmed God's work in and for you? In what ways would you like Him to?

4. How have you seen conflict that was tamed by the Spirit?

5. How have you seen conflict intensified by the Spirit's presence? What were the results?

6. Do you feel like an orphan, or like a child of God? Why?

7. If you have not experienced the power of the Spirit, what is holding you back?

THE MAKER

THE COMMUNICATOR

THE KING

THE SAVIOR

THE SPIRIT

THE GREAT GIVER

THE HEALER

THE SACRIFICE

THE NEW MAN

THE MESSENGER

THE BRIDEGROOM

THE BODY

06. THE GREAT GIVER

the sabbath

BIBLE TEXT: Thus the heavens and the earth, and all the host of them, were finished. And on the seventh day God ended His work which He had done, and He rested on the seventh day from all His work which He had done. Then God blessed the seventh day and sanctified it, because in it He rested from all His work which God had created and made. (Genesis 2:1-3)

PRESENTER'S NOTE:

Please see notes to presenter on pages 89, 98, and 101.
Review the discussion questions early.

the **GREAT GIVER** synopsis

In this message we will discover 1) that God created the world in six days, forming and filling its spaces with beauty, then rested on the seventh day and filled it with the blessing of His fellowship in presence; 2) that God enshrined the seventh day in His moral law as an eternal memorial of creation and salvation, both being the product solely of *God's* work and power; 3) that the Sabbath is inextricably connected with the cross of Christ and the new covenant, inviting us to rest by faith in Christ for our salvation; and 4) that New Testament Christianity was a Sabbath-keeping church. To engage in Sabbath rest is to rest by faith in Christ, to live within the intimacy of God's love as the reason for our existence, and therefore to remember our position of dependence on God as *The Great Giver* of all good things.

The Great Giver

Creation is God's love actualized in material form. Because "God is love" (1 John 4:16), it is in His nature to give and therefore to create others to share in the relational bliss He enjoys. That's why you exist, why I exist—to love and be loved.

That's all!

And that's a lot.

It is, in fact, nothing short of astounding, as we will see.

In this message we will explore our place in creation as human beings. More specifically, we will explore what it means to be human in relation to God as both our Creator and our Savior.

Let's begin with the Creation account of Genesis, starting with chapter one, verses 1-5:

> In the beginning God created the heavens and the earth. The earth was without form, and void; and darkness was on the face of the deep. And the Spirit of God was hovering over the face of the waters. Then God said, "Let there be light"; and there was light. And God saw the light, that it was good; and God divided the light from the darkness. God called the light Day, and the darkness He called Night. So the evening and the morning were the first day.

And with that, the story begins.

Our story begins.

As we take in the whole picture with one sweeping glance, we notice that the story of Creation unfolds with deliberate, poetic logic. Genesis 1:1 through 2:3 is, in fact, a beautifully crafted poem constructed in the literary form of a chiasm, which simply means, in this instance, that the story is told in the shape of a mountain, with the two sides ascending to one common pinnacle while mirroring one another with corresponding features.

A series of six literal days, each with an evening and a morning, compose the Creation event, followed by a seventh day of rest. That's the basic picture. But then we notice that day one corresponds to day four, day two corresponds to day five, day three corresponds to day six, and day seven occupies the focal point of the poem at the pinnacle of the chiasm.

> **PRESENTER:** *While giving the above explanation, you should either draw the following illustration on a board or show it as a PowerPoint image, or ask for seven volunteers from the audience to be arranged on the stage in the shape of an A, each one holding up their fingers or a sign to indicate which day they represent.*

As we read the Creation poem, we see God moving forward in an artistic pattern of *forming* and *filling*. On the first three days God *forms* spaces by dividing the material elements of creation. On the next three days God *fills* those spaces with beautiful things.

> **PRESENTER** *can use the following as an illustration written out on a board or as a PowerPoint graphic in order to build on the previous graphic.*

A. Day 1—God creates heaven and earth and separates the light from the darkness.

  B. Day 2—God separates the water and the sky.

    C. Day 3—God separates the land and the water.

      D. Day 7—God rests from His work and fills the seventh day with blessing.

    C. Day 6—God fills the land with animals and mankind.

  B. Day 5—God fills the water with fish and the sky with birds.

A. Day 4—God assigns the sun to the light and the moon to the darkness.

On day one God creates light and divides the light from the darkness, and then God loops back on day four to fill the light with the sun and the darkness with the moon.

On day two God forms the water and the sky into divided spaces, and then on day five He fills the water with fish and the sky with birds.

On day three God forms the land and the water into separate spaces, and then on day six He fills the land with plants, animals, and mankind. Also on day six, God forms the man from the dust of the ground and then fills the man with the breath of life.

And then, at the pinnacle of the chiasm, God rests from His work on the seventh day and fills it with blessing and sanctity. Genesis 2:1-3 beautifully expresses the climax of the chiasm:

> Thus the heavens and the earth, and all the host of them, were finished. And on the seventh day God ended His work which He had done, and He rested on the seventh day from all His work which He had done. [3] Then God blessed the seventh day and sanctified it, because in it He rested from all His work which God had created and made.

> The seventh day is the most unique space of all because it is not a physical space composed of matter but rather a relational space composed of time. And this space is not filled with more material elements, but with the blessing of God's fellowshipping presence. Thus the chiastic structure of the poem points to the blessing of fellowship with God as the grand objective of Creation and to the seventh day as the recurring space in time where that fellowship is most intimately realized. The seventh day is a constant reminder, then, of the relational love toward which the entire creative process was reaching.

Now that we have the basic picture before us, let's back up and focus in on what the Creation story reveals regarding the character of God and humanity's blessed position in relation to God.

A fun way to get there is to imagine the first few moments of human consciousness. Genesis 2:7 begins to paint the picture for us:

> God formed man from the dust of the ground, and breathed into his nostrils the breath of life, and man became a living soul.

As the life force moves from the Creator into the man, oxygen floods his lungs. His eyes open, blink, and focus. God's face is just inches away. Creator and creature make eye contact. Imagine what that first introduction must have been like. Perhaps:

Hi, I'm God, your Maker.

Uh, hi, I'm. . .well. . .um. . .I don't know who I am.

You are Adam, the first human being I've made. Welcome to existence/reality/life.

Thanks! I quite like it. What's next?

What's next? Well. . .

What's next, indeed! God isn't done. Creation is not yet complete. Something, or rather, someone, is missing. So God gets playful with Adam in order to lead him into the realization of his need for a companion. Notice Genesis 2:18-22:

> And the Lord God said, "It is not good that man should be alone; I will make him a helper comparable to him." Out of the ground the Lord God formed every beast of the field and every bird of the air, and brought them to Adam to see what he would call them. And whatever Adam called each living creature, that was its name.

Can you see Adam standing there in bewilderment as the animals parade before him by twos, male and female? Gradually it begins to dawn on him that he has no romantic chemistry with any of the animals. With divine humor, verse 20 says:

> So Adam gave names to all cattle, to the birds of the air, and to every beast of the field. But for Adam there was not found a helper comparable to him.

Adam just could not see himself in a long term relationship with Mrs. Giraffe or Mrs. Chimpanzee. So in response to Adam's longing for a female companion that would be his equal, God created the woman. Verses 21 and 22:

> And the Lord God caused a deep sleep to fall on Adam, and he slept; and He took one of his ribs, and closed up the flesh in its place. Then the rib which the Lord God had taken from man He made into a woman, and He brought her to the man.

There they stand before their Maker, the first man and the first woman, Adam and Eve. Their minds are processing every sight and sound and aroma around them. Their senses are flooded with sheer pleasure. Every cell of their bodies is alive with pulsating energy as they give themselves to one another in the perfect environment of Eden. Now that the man and the woman both exist, living with selfless love each for the other, the image of God is reproduced and Creation is complete.

But now we notice another feature of the story that holds great revelatory power regarding who God is and who we are in relation to God:

Adam and Eve were created on the sixth day of Creation, and on the latter part of the sixth day, after all the work of Creation was "finished." This means, of course, that:

1. Creation was (and is) a sheer gift from God.

2. Humanity's natural position is one of faith in God as *The Great Giver*.

They did not participate in the work of Creation, nor did they witness God perform the task of creating anything. They awoke to life as objects of grace, recipients of life and all its pleasures as a free gift. Then they rested on the seventh day as their first full day of life. There was nothing to which either the man or the woman could point and say, *There, do you see that beautiful thing, I made it*. Or even, *There, do you see that animal, that tree, that flower, God and I created that together*.

No!

The embedded truth of the seventh day is that Creation is "His work" alone and our primary position is that of restful dependence. God's primary role as the Creator is that of *Giver*, while the human position as creature is that of *Receiver*. Adam and Eve came to life in a position of faith and dependence. The necessity of trust was built into their ontological existence from the start.

It is easy to see that faith was intrinsic to pre-fall human existence. Adam and Eve find themselves alive by no effort of their own, in a world they had nothing to do with creating, face to face with a Being who is telling them a story. Maybe God said something like, "I made you from the dust of the ground under your feet, which I made from nothing at all but My own thoughts and feelings expressed through My words. You are perfect, exactly what I had in mind, and all this beauty that surrounds you is My gift to you." Whatever God said, the bottom line is that a glorious being stands before them claiming to be their Maker. To have any sense of identity they must believe that what God is telling them is indeed the case. They did not witness creation coming into being. All the "work" was "done" by the time the man and the woman open their eyes to life. They must simply trust that what they're being told is the truth. Their very existence is a faith experience, and the Sabbath day was instituted by God as a day of rest and reflection designed to keep fresh in their memory His love as *The Great Giver* and their blessed position as *Receivers*.

And this is what the Sabbath continues to mean throughout Scripture, taking on specific significance with regards to our salvation as God's work just as Creation in the beginning was His work.

Trace the biblical thread with me.

Moral Law

As we move forward in the biblical narrative, we discover that the Sabbath is a part of God's great moral law, the Ten Commandments. This is extremely significant, of course, because it means that the Sabbath is not an arbitrary rule imposed upon creation, but rather an integral part of its moral fabric. As such, the Sabbath is universal and eternal for all human beings. It is the fourth commandment of the ten.

Let's read it in Exodus 20:8-11:

> Remember the Sabbath day, to keep it holy. Six days you shall labor and do all your work, but the seventh day is the Sabbath of the Lord your God. In it you shall do no work: you, nor your son, nor your daughter, nor your male servant, nor your female servant, nor your cattle, nor your stranger who is within your gates. For in six days the Lord made the heavens and the earth, the sea, and all that is in them, and rested the seventh day. Therefore the Lord blessed the Sabbath day and hallowed it.

We are quick to notice that all of the other commandments are of a moral nature. We readily acknowledge, for example, that the sixth commandment, which forbids murder, and the seventh commandment, which forbids adultery, are necessary moral laws that apply to all human beings for all time. Of course this is the case. According to Jesus, love is the summation of God's law. It is easy to see that love would preclude committing murder or being unfaithful to one's marriage vows. But what about the fourth commandment, the one regarding the Sabbath? Is it, like the other nine commandments, an imperative moral law intrinsic to the operations of love?

Emphatically, *yes!*

If God's law is a description of what love looks like in action, then Sabbath keeping must, in some way, constitute an enactment of love and therefore must be of a moral character. This is easy to see when we remember the meaning of the Sabbath as indicated in the Genesis account of Creation.

First, we saw that the Sabbath was made holy by God and was filled with the blessing of God's fellowshipping presence. Secondly, we saw that the Sabbath signifies our proper relation to God as creatures of dependence who must necessarily live by faith toward our Creator if we are to know Him as the God of love that He is. The Sabbath, then, occupies the role of a memorial. It reminds us that God created the heavens and earth, and that God created mankind in His image to be active participants in His love.

Both of these points are, without question, of moral significance. When I keep the Sabbath I am acknowledging God as my Creator and Sustainer, engaging in a tangible relational action that communicates to Him that I am living in restful dependence upon Him rather than rebelliously venturing out in self-dependence. So yes, the inclusion of the Sabbath in God's moral law makes perfect sense. To know God as *The Great Giver* of all good things and to relate to Him as such with faith and love is, in fact, the highest moral state of the human being.

Paul gets to the heart of what sin is when he declares, "Whatever is not of faith is sin" (Romans 14:23). All sin, whatever behavioral form it takes, amounts to broken trust, relational failure, or disengagement from faithful love for God and others. The Sabbath commandment is the one among the ten that brings faith into our keeping of all the other commandments. It is the one that tells us as created beings that we are utterly dependent on God as our Creator.

We conclude, then, that the Sabbath is definitely part of the moral structure of life as God created life to function. It is a recurring space in time that memorializes the proper nature of our relationship with God. Each week it comes to me, to you, to every human being, and speaks the truth of who we are and who God is to us.

A Memorial of Creation and Redemption

Okay, so we've seen that the Sabbath is set forth in Scripture as a memorial of the fact that creation is God's work and therefore a pure gift to humanity. Now we turn our attention to the fact that the Sabbath is also a memorial of salvation as God's work as well, given to human beings as a free gift in Christ.

We launch into this part of our study by taking note of the enlightening fact that the Bible contains two versions of God's law, the first version recorded in Exodus 20 and the second in Deuteronomy 5. As we examine the two versions, we discover that all of the commandments are essentially the same, except for the fourth commandment, the one regarding the Sabbath. In the Exodus 20 version of the law, as we have already read, the Sabbath is set forth as a memorial of creation. But in the Deuteronomy 5 version of the Ten Commandments, Creation is not mentioned in the Sabbath commandment. Rather, in this case the Sabbath is set forth as a memorial of deliverance and liberation. Let's read it in Deuteronomy 5:12-15:

> Observe the Sabbath day, to keep it holy, as the Lord your God commanded you. Six days you shall labor and do all your work, but the seventh day is the Sabbath of the Lord your God. In it you shall do no work: you, nor your son, nor your daughter, nor your male servant, nor your female servant, nor your ox, nor your donkey, nor any of your cattle, nor your stranger who is within your gates, that your male servant and your female servant may rest as well as you. And remember that you were a slave in the land of Egypt, and the Lord your God brought you out from there by a mighty hand and by an outstretched arm; therefore the Lord your God commanded you to keep the Sabbath day.

In the Exodus 20 version of God's Law, the rationale for the Sabbath is God's finished work of Creation. But in the Deuteronomy 5 version of God's law, the rationale for the Sabbath is that it operates as a memorial of the work God achieved in delivering Israel from bondage in Egypt. But how can the Sabbath function as a memorial of these two very different events? The answer lies in the fact that these two events aren't that different after all. Both were achieved by the mighty power of God without any human contribution.

And that's the point!

How did God deliver Israel from Egyptian bondage? Deuteronomy 5 gives the answer:

> God brought you out from there by a mighty hand and by an outstretched arm; therefore the Lord your God commanded you to keep the Sabbath day.

The language here—*by a mighty hand and by an outstretched arm*—is intended to convey the idea that their liberation was achieved by a divine exertion of energy, not by their own power. The parallel with Creation is obvious and perfect. God created the world in six days by His own creative energy and now God delivers from bondage, just the same, by His own mighty power.

Now, of course, the historic event referred to is none other than the Exodus, and the Passover event was the point of deliverance for Israel. The lamb was slain and its blood was painted above and on either side of each Israelite door. As the angel of death passed through Egypt to slay each family's firstborn, every Israelite home marked by the blood was passed over. That night, the children of Israel walked free by virtue of the blood of the lamb.

But to what future events did the blood of the lamb point? Referring to the death of Jesus on the cross, in 1 Corinthians 5:7 the apostle Paul says, "Christ, our Passover, was sacrificed for us."

So the cross of Christ is explicitly memorialized in the Deuteronomy 5 version of the Sabbath commandment. The liberation of Israel from Egyptian bondage pointed forward to the liberation of humanity from its bondage to sin, to be achieved by the mighty outpouring of divine love in the sacrifice of Christ at Calvary. The Sabbath tells us the truth of God's finished work of salvation in Christ as much as it tells us of God's finished work of Creation. In fact, we discover in Scripture a deliberate parallel between Creation and salvation.

The Creation Salvation Parallel

With John's Gospel, the New Testament opens its storyline with a direct parallel to the opening verses of the Old Testament. In this way John points us to Creation as a passageway to understanding salvation. Notice the comparison:

Genesis 1:1-3:
In the beginning God created the heavens and the earth. The earth was without form, and void; and darkness was on the face of the deep. And the Spirit of God was hovering over the face of the waters. Then God said, "Let there be light"; and there was light.

John 1:1-5:
In the beginning was the Word, and the Word was with God, and the Word was God. He was in the beginning with God. All things were made through Him, and without Him nothing was made that was made. In Him was life, and the life was the light of men. And the light shines in the darkness, and the darkness did not overcome it.

Two distinct but converging narratives are here initiated: the story of Creation and the story of Redemption. As both Creator and Redeemer, Jesus is the active agent in both stories. Each story also begins with the necessity of light shinning forth in the darkness, and Jesus is the light source in both instances. In 2 Corinthians 4:6, Paul picks up the significance of the parallel: "For God, who said, 'Let light shine out of darkness,' made His light shine in our hearts to give us the light of the knowledge of the glory of God in the face of Christ."

Repeatedly in Scripture salvation is articulated with "Creation language." Here are a few powerful examples:

2 Corinthians 5:17:

Therefore, if anyone is in Christ, he is a new creation; old things have passed away; behold, all things have become new.

Ephesians 2:8-10:

For by grace you have been saved through faith, and that not of yourselves; it is the gift of God, not of works, lest anyone should boast. For we are His workmanship, created in Christ Jesus for good works, which God prepared beforehand that we should walk in them.

Ephesians 4:23-24

Be renewed in the spirit of your mind, and that you put on the new man which was created according to God, in true righteousness and holiness.

Psalm 51:10-12:

Create in me a clean heart, O God, and renew a steadfast spirit within me. . . Restore to me the joy of Your salvation.

In each of these Scriptures salvation is spoken of as God performing a new work of creation. And that's precisely what salvation is—the creation of a new humanity in Christ.

As we return to John's Gospel, we see that the creation/salvation parallel continues to completion. As Jesus comes to the close of His salvation mission, His prayer to the Father invokes the Sabbath language of Genesis 2. Notice His words in John 17:4: "I have glorified You on the earth. I have finished the work which You have given Me to do."

Back in Genesis 2 we read about the *finished work* of Creation. But now Jesus is speaking about the *finished work* of salvation. Then when Jesus comes to the cross, hanging between heaven and earth, He again invokes the Sabbath language of a finished work. John 19:30: "He said, 'It is finished!' And bowing His head, He gave up His spirit."

With poetic intentionality, Jesus cried out, "It is finished," on the latter half of the sixth day (Friday). He then died, having finished the work of redemption, resting in the tomb on the seventh day (Saturday), and rose to life again on the first day of the week (Sunday). By His death on the cross Jesus confirmed and immortalized the Sabbath as an eternal memorial of His salvation work.

> **PRESENTER *can simply mention at this point that Luke's chronology of the closing events of Christ's life, in Luke 23:54 through 24:3, informs us that Jesus finished the work of salvation on Friday, rested in the tomb on the Sabbath, and rose from the dead on Sunday.***

We see, then, that the Sabbath is a memorial of both Creation and salvation. It is God's weekly reminder to us that our salvation is 100 percent the gift of His grace, totally His accomplishment and not ours, to be received into our hearts by faith alone. As such the Sabbath guards us against legalism and self-dependence and lodges all our hope and trust in Jesus. The Sabbath tells us that good works contribute absolutely nothing to our salvation, while at the same time revealing God's mighty recreative work in us. We are saved by His creative work, not by our own works. Our part is to rest by faith in His mighty power to save us.

The Sabbath and the New Covenant

It makes total theological sense, then, that the Sabbath is set forth in Scripture as a new covenant memorial of our salvation in Christ. Isaiah 56:1-7 is a stunning prophecy of the Messiah and the establishment of the New Testament church:

> Thus says the LORD: "Keep justice, and do righteousness, for My salvation is about to come, and My righteousness to be revealed. 2Blessed is the man who does this,

and the son of man who lays hold on it; who keeps from defiling the Sabbath, and keeps his hand from doing any evil." [3]Do not let the son of the foreigner who has joined himself to the LORD Speak, saying, "The LORD has utterly separated me from His people"; nor let the eunuch say, "Here I am, a dry tree." [4]For thus says the LORD: "To the eunuchs who keep My Sabbaths, and choose what pleases Me, and hold fast My covenant, [5]even to them I will give in My house and within My walls a place and a name better than that of sons and daughters; I will give them an everlasting name that shall not be cut off. [6]Also the sons of the foreigner who join themselves to the LORD, to serve Him, and to love the name of the LORD, to be His servants—everyone who keeps from defiling the Sabbath, and holds fast My covenant— [7]even them I will bring to My holy mountain, and make them joyful in My house of prayer. Their burnt offerings and their sacrifices will be accepted on My altar; for My house shall be called a house of prayer for all nations."

In this Messianic prophecy, five points are evident:

1. The Messiah will bring God's "salvation" to our world.

2. A blessing is pronounced upon anyone who "lays hold on it," on the salvation of the Messiah, that is, and in the same sentence those who lay hold on the salvation of Christ also keep "the Sabbath."

3. Isaiah foretells that the Messiah's salvation is for all, not only for Jews, but for Gentiles too—"the son of the foreigner who has joined Himself to the Lord" and "the eunuchs."

4. Then, with crystal clarity, Isaiah foretells that these New Testament Gentile believers will be Sabbath keepers as they lay hold of the Messiah's covenant.

5. As a result, the Church of Christ will be established for all nations: *My house shall be called a house of prayer for all nations.*

According to this prophecy, New Testament believers, both Jews and non-Jews, will be Sabbath keepers because the Sabbath signifies the new covenant. This makes perfect sense in the light of what we have discovered concerning the meaning of the Sabbath as a memorial of both Creation and salvation. Now we see that the Sabbath is inextricably connected with the new covenant, which, according to Scripture, involves God writing His law of love upon the hearts of all who put their trust in Christ, thus ruling out any and all possibility of salvation by works. The Sabbath stands as an eternal memorial of the free salvation we have by faith alone in Jesus Christ.

It is not surprising, then, to find that the New Testament Church, both Jews and Gentiles, were Sabbath keepers. As we come to the book of Acts, we read that this was exactly the case. In Acts 13, please notice the practice of Paul and his posse of evangelistic workers. Verses 13-15:

> Now when Paul and his party set sail from Paphos, they came to Perga in Pamphylia; and John, departing from them, returned to Jerusalem. But when they departed from Perga, they came to Antioch in Pisidia, and went into the synagogue on the Sabbath day and sat down. And after the reading of the Law and the Prophets, the rulers of the synagogue sent to them, saying, "Men and brethren, if you have any word of exhortation for the people, say on."

So here we have Paul and his friends keeping the Sabbath as New Testament believers. Now someone will say, of course Paul kept the Sabbath, because he was a Jew. But let's keep reading.

At this point Paul preached a powerful new covenant sermon regarding the death and resurrection of Christ, forgiveness of sin, and justification by faith alone in Christ (Verses 16-41).

Then what happened? Let's read verses 42-44:

> So when the Jews went out of the synagogue, the Gentiles begged that these words might be preached to them the next Sabbath. Now when the congregation had broken up, many of the Jews and devout proselytes followed Paul and Barnabas, who, speaking to them, persuaded them to continue in the grace of God. On the next Sabbath almost the whole city came together to hear the word of God.

Notice that the Gentile believers did not come to Paul as he finished his Sabbath sermon in the Jewish house of worship and schedule him to preach to their non-Jewish congregation on Sunday, but rather they scheduled him for "the next Sabbath." Clearly, all of these New Testament believers, Jews and Gentiles alike, were Sabbath keepers. Of course they were, just as the prophecy of Isaiah 56 said they would be. According to the book of Acts, the Apostolic Church was a Sabbath keeping church.

It wasn't until some two centuries after the apostolic period that Sunday, the day revered by pagan sun worshipers in the Roman Empire, began to be introduced into Christianity along with various other departures from the new covenant faith of the early church. The Sabbath, which, as we have seen, was given by God as a powerful memorial of Christ our Creator and Christ our Savior, was gradually abandoned by the church as she sunk into long, dark ages of apostasy. Sunday observance became the practice of Romanized "Christianity" in keeping with its system of salvation by works in high-handed apostasy against the gospel of salvation by grace alone through faith alone in Christ. That's a brief history of how Sunday observance was introduced into Christianity and the Sabbath was lost sight of. More details of this history are forthcoming in one of our future messages.

In this present message we have discovered:

1. That God created the world in six days, forming and filling its spaces with beautiful things, and then God rested on the seventh day and filled it with the blessing of His fellowship in presence.

2. That God enshrined the seventh day in His moral law as an eternal memorial of Creation and salvation, both being the product of His work and power rather than our own.

3. That the Sabbath is inextricably connected with the cross of Christ and the new covenant, inviting us to rest by faith in Christ for our salvation.

4. And that New Testament Christianity was a Sabbath keeping church.

5. To engage in Sabbath rest is to rest by faith in Christ, to live within the intimacy of God's love as the reason for our existence, and therefore to remember our position of dependence on God as *The Great Giver* of all good things.

I invite you, dear friend, to begin meeting with your Creator and Savior, Jesus Christ, each Sabbath day as a constant reminder that you can rest by faith in the salvation He has given you as the free gift of His grace.

Please pray with me.

HELPFUL TIPS

PRESENTER: *For this message you should strongly consider engaging the congregation in some form of tangible commitment to become Sabbath keepers: a raising of hands as you pray, coming forward as you pray, or a response card.*

PRESENTER, PLEASE SHARE WITH YOUR AUDIENCE THAT THIS IS A SAFE ZONE.
It's a safe place to be themselves. • Everyone has the right to their own opinion.
There are no dumb questions. • All comments are encouraged and respected.

Discussion Questions

1. What was your reaction to the Creation story as given in this message?

2. Had you heard before of the concept that three days were used in "forming," and three in "filling"?

3. Have you been exposed to the idea of the seventh-day Sabbath, and if so, was it as a gift of rest, or as a legalistic burden? Discuss.

4. When the Sabbath is treated legalistically, does that attitude conflict with the Sabbath's role in memorializing the fact that God alone is responsible both for Creation and for re-creation or salvation? How could you deflect this latter attitude?

5. Does anything need to change in your life in order for you to enter fully into God's free gift of salvation?

6. How could accepting the free gift of Sabbath rest help with that?

HELP YOUR YOUTH GROUP GROW CLOSER TO GOD

FREE DOWNLOAD AVAILABLE AT

HTTP://WWW.GCYOUTHMINISTRIES.ORG

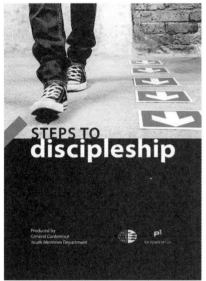

THE MAKER

THE COMMUNICATOR

THE KING

THE SAVIOR

THE SPIRIT

THE GREAT GIVER

THE HEALER

THE SACRIFICE

THE NEW MAN

THE MESSENGER

THE BRIDEGROOM

THE BODY

07. THE HEALER
healthful living

BIBLE TEXT: The thief does not come except to steal, and to kill, and to destroy. I have come that they may have life, and that they may have it more abundantly. (John 10:10)

PRESENTER'S NOTE: On page 111 you will be asked to insert a personal testimony about God's miraculous and wonderful healing of a family member, friend, or even yourself. Prepare your testimony early.

the **HEALER** synopsis

Jesus' stated mission was one in which the needs—physical, emotional, spiritual, and social—of broken, hurting people were of absolutely central importance. Jesus was a healer—a healer of bodies, of hearts, and of relationships. Where He went, healing and restoration followed in His wake. The love of God flowed out from Him to all who came near. This message, then, deals with three important questions: Is all disease caused by Satan? (Yes, in its original sense, no on an individual level—we and the planet are broken now.) Why doesn't Jesus heal everyone? (He will, eventually—every trusting person.) How can I cooperate with and spread Jesus' healing ministry? (We can learn to live in a way that cares for our bodies and souls as close as possible to the way God originally intended, before sin. And we can share that!)

The Healer

According to the record we have in the Gospels of Jesus' life, He spent as much time healing as He did preaching—maybe even more. The blind, the lame, and the diseased all received His special attention and care. Casting cultural and societal norms aside, He even *touched* those who were considered unclean and cursed. On more than one occasion He performed the greatest conceivable act of healing: that is, He raised the dead back to life!

This healing dimension of Jesus' ministry should not surprise us.

After all, God is love. And Jesus was God's love on full display in human form. Of course He would heal! Of course He would touch!

In what some have called His "Nazareth Manifesto," Jesus, quoting Isaiah, announced His life's purpose (Luke 4:16-19):

> So He came to Nazareth, where He had been brought up. And as His custom was, He went into the synagogue on the Sabbath day, and stood up to read. And He was handed the book of the prophet Isaiah. And when He had opened the book, He found the place where it was written:
>
> The Spirit of the LORD is upon Me,
> Because He has anointed Me
> To preach the gospel to the poor;
> He has sent Me to heal the brokenhearted,
> To proclaim liberty to the captives
> And recovery of sight to the blind,
> To set at liberty those who are oppressed;
> To proclaim the acceptable year of the LORD.

To heal!

To restore!

To release!

To proclaim!

Jesus' stated mission was one in which the needs—physical, emotional, spiritual, and social—of broken, hurting people were of absolutely central importance. Jesus was a healer—a healer of bodies, of hearts, and of relationships. Where He went, healing and restoration followed in His wake. The love of God flowed out from Him to all who came near.

Later in this same chapter, Luke 4, Jesus heals Peter's mother-in-law. Verse 39 says He, "rebuked the fever." Don't miss that! It's a critical point. Jesus, here, did not treat illness and sickness as somehow fitting into God's great plan, but as an enemy to be rebuked. The very next verse reads:

> When the sun was setting, all those who had any that were sick with various diseases brought them to Him; and He laid His hands on every one of them and healed them.

Sometimes something *more than physical* was taking place. Jesus's healing ministry was displacing demonic forces from people and places. Notice the next verse:

> And demons also came out of many, crying out and saying, "You are the Christ, the Son of God!" And He, rebuking them, did not allow them to speak, for they knew that He was the Christ.

Notice here, again the word "rebuke" is used. Disease, according to Jesus the Healer, was a tool of the enemy, Satan. Later in Luke's Gospel, a particularly insightful account is recorded. It's found in chapter 13:10-17:

> Now He was teaching in one of the synagogues on the Sabbath. And behold, there was a woman who had a spirit of infirmity eighteen years, and was bent over and could in no way raise herself up. But when Jesus saw her, He called her to Him and said to her, "Woman, you are loosed from your infirmity." And He laid His hands on her, and immediately she was made straight, and glorified God. But the ruler of the synagogue answered with indignation, because Jesus had healed on the Sabbath; and he said to the crowd, "There are six days on which men ought to work; therefore come and be healed on them, and not on the Sabbath day." The Lord then answered him and said, "Hypocrite! Does not each one of you on the Sabbath loose his ox or donkey from the stall, and lead it away to water it? So ought not this woman, being a daughter of Abraham, whom Satan has bound—think of it—for eighteen years, be loosed from this bond on the Sabbath?" And when He said these things, all His adversaries were put to shame; and all the multitude rejoiced for all the glorious things that were done by Him.

Jesus here peels back the curtain that separates the seen from the unseen and reveals the true source of the woman's illness—"whom Satan has bound." These four short words unlock a deep and dark reality beyond. We know who this Satan is; we've already identified him in a previous presentation. He's the enemy, the accuser, a liar and a murderer. Jesus' words cannot be misunderstood here. He takes no responsibility for the woman's diseased condition. He says Satan bears that responsibility.

So Jesus' acts of healing were acts of war, acts of displacement.

And right here, on this point, we encounter a profoundly important parable in which Jesus sought to explain His healing and restoring ministry. We'll stay in Luke and turn back two chapters, to chapter 11.

Just after casting out a demon, Jesus is accused by His doubters and detractors of possessing the power to do so by being in league with "Beelzebub, the ruler of the demons" (v. 15). Jesus then tries to reason with them and concludes His reasoning with a parable:

> When a strong man, fully armed, guards his own palace, his goods are in peace.
> But when a stronger than he comes upon him and overcomes him, he takes from
> him all his armor in which he trusted, and divides his spoils (vs. 21, 22).

Whoa!

So *that's* what's happening?

Jesus is clearly the One (*The One!*) who is "stronger than he." Stronger than who? The enemy, Satan. Jesus here is describing acts of war and displacement, whereby He is reclaiming, through His healing ministry, people from the enemy's power and control.

So we repeat: Jesus's acts of healing were acts of war, acts of displacement!

This biblical picture raises many questions and issues. Let's address three of them.

1. Is all disease caused by Satan?

2. Why doesn't Jesus heal everyone?

3. How can I cooperate with and spread Jesus' healing ministry?

1. *Is all disease caused by Satan?*

The answer to this question is both *yes* and *no*.

The answer is *yes* in the sense that Satan is the *originator* of all disease, since his rebellion was the initial rebellion against God and His love. Jesus made this very point when, in John 8:44, He declared that:

> He was a murderer from the beginning, and does not stand in the truth, because there is no truth in him. When he speaks a lie, he speaks from his own resources, for he is a liar and the father of it.

Jesus fingers Satan as "the father" of lies (and all other evils) and his rebellion, as "the beginning" of evil (murder, for example).

So in the sense of origins and ultimate beginnings, yes, *all* disease comes from Satan. This does not mean, though, that every instance of disease, pain, or death is the result of Satan's direct intervention. This is an important distinction that must be grasped: the origin of disease is directly traceable to Satan's rebellion against God's government of love and freedom; however, this does not mean that every instance or occurrence of disease is from his hand.

Let's try and understand this point a little better still.

As we've learned, when Adam and Eve forfeited their position as managers and stewards of earth, Satan became "the ruler of this world" (John 12:31; 14:30; 16:11). The earth itself, following Adam and Eve's abdication, was cursed and, as such, actually *changed* at some fundamental level. The earth itself was placed in bondage.

Recall the parable of the wheat and tares (Matthew 13:24-30), which we've considered in a previous presentation. A landowner sowed good seed in his field. Tares appeared. The landowner's workers questioned him about the presence of the tares. He responded with unmistakable clarity: "He said unto them, 'An enemy hath done this'" (v. 28).

These five words—an enemy has done this—remind us of those four crucially important words from the story of the healed woman in Luke 13: "whom Satan has bound."

What a difference nine words can make!

Jesus makes it indisputably clear here that the presence of tares, which in context are "the sons of the wicked one" (v. 38), that is, *evil things*, was not God's intention or plan. Jesus, in the parable, takes no responsibility for the presence of the tares. Neither did He take responsibility for the woman's diseased condition in the temple. In both cases, He laid the blame squarely where it belonged:

Four words: *whom Satan has bound.*

Five words: *an enemy has done this.*

John helps us to better grasp this broken-people and broken-world picture when he says, "the whole world lies under the sway of the wicked one" (1 John 5:19).

Again we see, in a very real sense, this world is Satan's territory. It is broken. It is confused. It is filled with pain, death, and disease. In a deep and remarkable passage on the earth's bondage and brokenness, Paul writes:

> For the earnest expectation of the *creation* eagerly waits for the revealing of the sons of God.
>
> For the creation was subjected to futility, not willingly, but because of Him who subjected it in hope;
>
> because the *creation* itself also will be delivered from the bondage of corruption into the glorious liberty of the children of God.
>
> For we know that the *whole creation* groans and labors with birth pangs together until now. (Romans 8:19-22)

Notice that Paul speaks of "creation" in each of these verses. What does he say about it? It is waiting for redemption. It was subjected to futility in hope. It is under the bondage of corruption. It groans with labor pains even up to the present time.

What a picture! The earth itself is in trouble! In bondage! In the pains of promised new life to come!

We can summarize this simply: *the earth is broken.* And so are the people who live here. Our bodies are broken; our hearts are broken; our families are broken; our spirits are broken.

We need a healer! And Jesus is The One!

Let's move now to our second question.

2. Why doesn't Jesus heal everyone?

The answer to this might sound a little strange at first, but here it goes: *Jesus will heal all those who put their trust in Him.*

Not some, not most, but *all*.

"But, wait a minute," you might be thinking, "I've had a friend or family member who's been sick for many years, and they believe in Jesus, but they're still not healed. How can you say that?"

The answer resides in the great biblical truth of the resurrection, which we'll cover in our next presentation. But, briefly, the truth is that God will redeem, restore, and completely heal—body, mind, and spirit—all those who put their trust in Him, who believe and trust in Jesus the Messiah's faithfulness.

Scripture speaks of believers receiving glorified bodies (Philippians 3:21; 1 Corinthians 15:50-55). These are bodies free from sickness and disease. They are healed, whole, and healthy. They are the promised inheritance of every believer!

God, at times, still heals people in miraculous and wonderful ways today!

But even if a believer is not healed bodily here and now, the promise is absolutely sure: *they will be healed in the resurrection!*

Listen to the praise of the ancient psalmist in Psalm 103:1-5:

> Bless the LORD, O my soul; And all that is within me, bless His holy name
>
> Bless the LORD, O my soul, And forget not all His benefits:
>
> Who forgives all your iniquities, Who heals all your diseases,
>
> Who redeems your life from destruction, Who crowns you with lovingkindness tender mercies,
>
> Who satisfies your mouth with good things, So that your youth is renewed like the eagle's.

Note especially that phrase: "Who heals all your diseases."

Insert testimony here. Instructions on page 105

The promise is sure! You will be healed! All believers will be healed!

It may happen in the here-and-now, or it may happen in the hereafter. But the point is: it will happen! Jesus' resurrection guarantees it! We'll talk more about this in our next presentation, but now let's turn our attention to our third and final question.

3. *How can I cooperate with and spread Jesus' healing ministry?*

Sometimes God's cures and remedies don't come in the form of marvelous and miraculous healings. Sometimes they come through simply cooperating with Him in living healthy lives, by treating our bodies in the way He instructs us to.

Now here again, as with the answers to our first two questions, this might strike some of you as rather strange. After all, does God care about how I treat my body? What I eat and drink? And how much exercise I get?

The biblical answer is a resounding *yes!*

If this sounds strange to you, it's only because you've imbibed, with many others today, an incorrect idea called *anthropological dualism*. Now don't be afraid of those big words, because their meaning is actually very simple. It means that mankind is made of two parts: body and spirit. This is an old idea, traceable directly to the ancient Greeks who taught that reality was composed of either matter or spirit. Matter, they said, was bad and corrupt; but spirit was good and pure. Furthermore, they taught that matter was temporary, but spirit was eternal.

In future presentations, including our next one, we'll address these ancient and incorrect Greek ideas in more depth, and we will talk about how they found their way into Christian thinking. We'll also identify and affirm the biblically correct alternatives.

Many, even among Christians, have unwittingly imbibed this Greek dualistic view of reality. They think that God isn't really concerned with the body; what He cares about is our spirit. But Scripture says otherwise. God, in fact, cares very much about how we treat our bodies since, among other reasons, a healthy body and healthy mind go hand in hand.

Health is about more than six-pack abs, bulging biceps, and general physical fitness. Think of health as *wholeness*. A healthy person is a *whole* person. If someone has big biceps but a history of broken relationships, that person is not healthy, not biblically speaking. Speaking of Jesus' maturation, Luke wrote: *"And Jesus increased in wisdom and stature, and in favor with God and man"* (2:52).

Jesus was a whole person, a healthy, well-rounded person. Note the areas of growth and development:

Wisdom: intellectual health.

Stature: physical health.

Favor with God: spiritual health.

Favor with man: social health.

This is what it means to be healthy, to be whole. Part of health includes a healthy body. Notice Paul's language in 1 Corinthians:

> Or do you not know that your body is the temple of the Holy Spirit who is in you, whom you have from God, and you are not your own? For you were bought at a price; therefore glorify God in your body and in your spirit, which are God's. (6:19, 20)

> Therefore, whether you eat or drink, or whatever you do, do all to the glory of God. (10:31)

Well, that's pretty clear. Listen also to Romans 12:1, 2:

> I beseech you therefore, brethren, by the mercies of God, that you present your bodies a living sacrifice, holy, acceptable to God, which is your reasonable service.

One translation of this verse (NIV) says:

> Therefore, I urge you, brothers, in view of God's mercy, to offer your bodies as living sacrifices, holy and pleasing to God—this is your spiritual act of worship.

So the way I treat my body can be a spiritual act of worship? Yes, according to Scripture it can! Clearly, God is interested in how we treat our bodies. In fact, in a very real sense, they're not even our bodies! What did Scripture say? "You are not your own" and "glorify God in your body... which [is] God's."

When you think about it, this makes sense. After all, who gave you your body? Did you buy it? Find it? Earn it? No! You received it! From who? Ultimately, God, of course.

Not surprisingly then, God, as a loving and concerned parent, gives principles in Scripture regarding how we, *the children,* should eat and drink and live. These principles are rooted in God's original Eden plan for humanity and are simple and health-promoting.

1. The ideal and original diet was a vegetarian diet (Genesis 1:29). In his New York Times Best Seller, *In Defense of Food,* Michael Pollan summarizes the key to healthy eating in just seven simple words: "Eat food. Not too much. Mostly plants." There you have it! God's original diet, study after study continues to confirm, is a varied and largely, or entirely, vegetarian diet. After the flood, yes, God gave permission to eat animals, but only the clean ones. This distinction continues today as a health-giving principle from God. Clean mammals split the hoof and chew the cud. Clean water creatures have fins and scales. And clean birds are the chicken-like birds—not the birds of prey such as owls, hawks, and eagles. You can read it for yourself in Leviticus 11.

2. Alcoholic beverages are harmful to the body and can lead to drunkenness and addiction. On the whole, Scripture urges believers to stay away from that which, "at the last bites like a serpent, and stings like a viper" (Proverbs 23:32). Notice that it doesn't sting *at the first,* but "at the last." In Scripture Satan is repeatedly called a "serpent" because he is a deceiver (see Revelation 12:9). He lures you in with one thing, which looks tempting and enticing, but then he sinks his teeth of despair, guilt, shame, addiction, and sin into you. This is how alcohol works; it starts off fun, innocent, and alluring, but brings pain, shame, addiction, and death "at the last." No wonder Scripture also says, "Wine is a mocker and beer a brawler; whoever is led astray by them is not wise" (Proverbs 20:1, NIV). Alcohol and drugs contribute to so much of this world's pain and misery: child abuse, unwanted pregnancies, spousal abuse, poverty, murder, rape, drunk driving deaths, birth defects, and much more. Not only are they bad for society, they're bad for us as individuals. Believers will abstain from alcohol and other intoxicating and dangerous substances because they are already high on life and on God!

3. Exercise is critically important for optimum health, and while Scripture doesn't speak directly to the issue of the need for exercise, it's self-evidently the case that, in the words of one Christian writer, "the whole body is designed for action." Because of modern technology, many cultures today, on average, get very little necessary exercise.

If you're a farmer, or a tree cutter, or a shepherd, you get your exercise "on the job" so to speak. If you're not active during your job, then it's crucial that you make time to play, to exercise, to swim, to hike, or to run. To do something! More than any other single decision you can make, the decision to get regular exercise will increase your healthfulness and improve the quality of your physical life.

4. Finally, rest and fellowship. In our last presentation we spoke about the importance of the Sabbath and of the rest and joy it brings. Keeping God's Sabbath and fellowshipping with Him and His people will go a long way in keeping you socially, emotionally, psychologically, and even physically healthy!

So to summarize, how can you cooperate with and spread the healing ministry of Jesus?

1. Eat healthful foods.

2. Avoid alcohol and drugs.

3. Get exercise.

4. Rest in and fellowship with God and His followers, the church.

And then encourage others to do the same!

God's plan for you is health and happiness! It's not just His plan in the hereafter, but also in the here and now! Jesus, The Healer, said it best of all: "The thief does not come except to steal, and to kill, and to destroy. I have come that they may have life, and that they may have it more abundantly" (John 10:10).

Jesus came not only to bring years to our life, but life to our years! This is what an abundant life means! A life lived in love with God!

Satan, the enemy, is the thief. He takes life and happiness and brings death and disease instead. But Jesus' promise is sure: "I have come that they may have life, and that they may have it more abundantly."

Don't you want that abundant, healthy, and whole life—a life only He can truly give?

PRESENTER, PLEASE SHARE WITH YOUR AUDIENCE THAT THIS IS A SAFE ZONE.
It's a safe place to be themselves. • Everyone has the right to their own opinion.
There are no dumb questions. • All comments are encouraged and respected.

Discussion Questions

1. What is your reaction to the concept that Satan originated all ills? Is this new to you, or difficult to accept? Why?

2. Can you think of times when you or others you knew felt that a particular illness or injury was caused directly by the devil? Share the story.

3. Share stories of times when you or someone you love have not been healed, despite prayer and faith. Did prayer and faith still help? If so, how?

4. How do you respond to the idea that everyone who trusts God and chooses His way will be healed eventually? Does that comfort you? Seem unrealistic?

5. Have you been used to believing that God cares how you treat your body?

6. Do you agree that the mind and spirit are affected by physical health? How?

7. To recap the health tips given in the message: Eat healthful foods. Avoid alcohol and drugs. Get exercise. Rest in and fellowship with God and His followers, the church. Discuss with your group the ways in which you already do these things and what the results have been. Then share which areas you would like to improve. You may like to pray for each other to meet the goals you decide on. What other ways can you help each other?

Senior
Youth
Ministry

HANDBOOK

Introducing the revised *Senior Youth Ministry Handbook*
Available online at www.gcyouthministries.org

YOUTH MINISTRIES
DEPARTMENT

P1
THE POWER OF ONE

THE MAKER

THE COMMUNICATOR

THE KING

THE SAVIOR

THE SPIRIT

THE GREAT GIVER

THE HEALER

THE SACRIFICE

THE NEW MAN

THE MESSENGER

THE BRIDEGROOM

THE BODY

08. THE SACRIFICE
death, hell, and the cross

BIBLE TEXT: For He made Him who knew no sin to be sin for us, that we might become the righteousness of God in Him. (2 Corinthians 5:21)

PRESENTER'S NOTE: At the end of this sermon you should be ready to make an appeal for an acceptance of the sacrifice that Christ has made on our behalf, asking for hands to be raised to signify acceptance.

See page 134.

the SACRIFICE synopsis

This message examines the two types of death in the Bible: the first death, which is merely a temporary death of the body, and the second death, which destroys both the body and the soul, or *psyche*. In the first death, the person is unconscious, knows nothing, and has nothing to do with anything on earth; however, the spirit, or self, is preserved by God for resurrection. We are all bound for full, unveiled encounter with God. All will stand before His throne and see His face. This will bring the shock of full self-knowledge—fatal to those who have not fully taken into themselves the reality of Jesus' total and complete death, accepted in their place—blazing glory for eternity to those who have.

The Sacrifice

Strange as it may seem at first consideration, according to the Bible there are two distinct categories of death; said another way: that which we commonly call *death* is really no death at all compared to the ultimate death of which Scripture warns and from which Jesus saves.

Revelation 2:14 is a good place to start:

> He who has an ear, let him hear what the Spirit says to the churches. He who over-comes shall not be hurt by the second death.

From the language of this promise we can easily deduce that there are two types of death we humans face. Logic dictates that since there is something called "the second death," there must be something we might rightly call "the first death."

Simple enough, but what is the difference between the two?

In one simple, straightforward sentence, Jesus draws the vital distinction between the first death and the second death. Take a look at Matthew 10:28:

> Fear not them which kill the body, but are not able to kill the soul: but rather fear Him which is able to destroy both soul and body in hell.

So then, according to Jesus, the first death involves merely the physical death of the body. And Jesus regards this death so lightly that He says we shouldn't even be afraid of it. Why not? Well, as we will see shortly, because the first death is temporary. From it there is a resurrection. It's not ultimate. Not final.

By contrast, Jesus says that the second death involves the destruction of both the body and the soul. Okay, so what does that mean? Well, the Greek word that is here translated "soul" is *psyche*. The usage of this word by Jesus will become extremely important for us as our study proceeds. For now, we simply need to take note of the fact that the second death is more than merely physical death. Rather, by infinite contrast, the second death is the destruction of both the body and the *psyche*—that is, the annihilation of the entire person, including all of the psychological content of ones personhood, and from which there is no resurrection. There is one exception, however, as we will see.

With this basic biblical perspective before us, let's explore the first death and the second in greater detail.

The First Death

A person can die the first death from one of five basic causes:

1. Homicide

2. Suicide

3. Tragedy

4. Disease

5. Old age

But here's the most important thing you can ever learn about the first death: in a sense, it's not really death, not in any kind of final or ultimate sense. In keeping with the Hebrew Scriptures, Jesus called the first death "sleep." One example will suffice.

Jesus was asked to heal a sick little girl, but He arrived too late. As He came to the house, her family and friends were crying because she had died. Now pay close attention to how Jesus responded to the situation in Luke 8:52-55:

> Now all wept and mourned for her; but He said, "Do not weep; she is not dead, but sleeping." And they ridiculed Him, knowing that she was dead. But He put them all outside, took her by the hand and called, saying, "Little girl, arise." Then her spirit returned, and she arose immediately. And He commanded that she be given something to eat.

Notice Jesus did not merely say the girl was sleeping. He went a step further and said, "She is *not* dead." The reason the people ridiculed Him is because they were certain she was, in fact, dead. Jesus knew this, of course. But He was communicating to them a deeper insight: the girl had not died in the ultimate second-death sense, but merely in the first-death sense. In order to demonstrate His point, He proceeded to awaken the girl from her first-death sleep.

The reason Jesus likened the first death to sleep is because, like sleep, when a person dies the first death they cease to be conscious until they are resurrected. This is the consistent testimony of Scripture. Let's consider Ecclesiastes 9:5-6 as an example:

> For the living know that they will die; but the dead know nothing, and they have no more reward, for the memory of them is forgotten. Also their love, their

hatred, and their envy have now perished; nevermore will they have a share in anything done under the sun.

Then notice Ecclesiastes 12:7:

Then the dust will return to the earth as it was, and the spirit will return to God who gave it.

These two Scriptures clearly indicate at least four vital points:

1. When a person dies the first death, they "know nothing." They are unconscious.

2. When a person dies the first death, because they are unconscious, they cease to have anything to do with anything in this world. Clearly, then, the dead do not communicate nor interact with the living.

3. When a person dies, their body returns to the dust. This is a poetic way of saying that the body decomposes.

4. Simultaneously, "the spirit returns to God who gave it." In other words, the individual identity—ones personality and character—is preserved by God for the resurrection.

Clearly, then, the first death is merely a physical cessation of conscious life, and from the first death there is a resurrection. What, then, is the second death?

The Second Death

To answer this question, let's return to Matthew 10:28, in which Jesus distinguished between the first death and the second death:

Fear not them which kill the body, but are not able to kill the soul: but rather fear Him which is able to destroy both soul and body in hell.

Here Jesus depicts the second death as the destruction of "both soul and body," and then He equates this destruction of the whole person with "hell." So when we are answering the question, *What is the second death?* we are also answering the question, *What is the biblical meaning of hell?* This is vitally important, because Jesus essentially says that hell is the destruction of "both soul and body," contrary to the popular notion that hell is an eternally *undestroyed* state in which souls live on and suffer without end.

Let's dig deeper.

You will recall that the Greek word here translated "soul" is *psyche*. The translators of the New Testament would have achieved greater clarity by simply translating the word as *mind*. That's what the word means and that's what Jesus was referring to.

So Jesus is clearly communicating that the second death involves the destruction of the whole person, both body and mind, whereas the first death merely involves the death of the body while the mind is preserved by God for the resurrection of the body, as we saw in Ecclesiastes 12:7. The "soul" in the New Testament English usage refers to the inner person and all it includes—the moral identity, personality, character, intellect, and emotions. This is what Paul calls, in Ephesians 3:16, "the inner man." As we have already seen, there is no consciousness of the "soul" apart from the body, but there is, nevertheless, an inner dimension to human nature that is preserved by God when a person dies the first death. We might say that God remembers or maintains a record of the unique identity or character of each of us when we die the first death. Therefore, in the resurrection, each individual will be exactly the same person they were before passing into the unconscious sleep of the first death.

Okay, so the second death, by contrast to the first, does not occur on merely a physical level, but rather on the level of the *psyche*, as well. Now let's delve deeper into the second death. Brace yourself.

In Revelation 20 we encounter the second death with chilling and vivid clarity. Follow the points carefully. Revelation 20:11-14:

> Then I saw a great white throne and Him who sat on it, from whose face the earth and the heaven fled away. And there was found no place for them. And I saw the dead, small and great, standing before God, and books were opened. And another book was opened, which is the Book of Life. And the dead were judged according to their works, by the things which were written in the books. The sea gave up the dead who were in it, and Death and Hades delivered up the dead who were in them. And they were judged, each one according to his works. Then Death and Hades were cast into the lake of fire. This is the second death.

What a heartbreaking and horrific depiction of the final demise of the wicked!

First of all, we see that those who are irrevocably evil—called "the wicked" in Scripture—are brought face to face with God. The second death is initiated by a full revelation of God seated upon "a great white throne" with His "face" fully exposed to the astonished gaze of all. This is super significant in Scripture. Once when Moses asked to see God's face, this is the answer God gave him in Exodus 34:20: "You cannot see My face; for no man shall see Me, and live."

What?!

So merely looking upon God's face would have a lethal effect on us?

Why? And in what sense?

Well, the answer is quite simple and self-evident. The reason why fallen human beings cannot see the face of God and survive the encounter is not because God is hostile but because God is pure love and we are selfish and sinful by contrast. To see God in all His perfect love and purity would react in the human mind to produce complete self-awareness. In the light of His holiness, we would see our own impure selfishness by contrast. And according to Revelation 20, this is precisely the encounter the wicked will have with God.

Now we are beginning to understand why Jesus said that the *psyche* is involved in the second death.

It is inevitable that every created being will encounter their Maker. In this sense, the ultimate destiny of each person, both the saved and the lost, is exactly the same. We are all bound for full, unveiled encounter with God. All will stand before His throne and see His face. But there will be a difference in the outcome of that encounter for the saved and the lost. Those who have trusted in Jesus will have been healed of their guilt by His forgiving mercy. They will see infinite love and acceptance in the face of God. There will be no unresolved shame inside of them to ignite with consciousness in His holy presence.

But the wicked, as they stand before God's throne, will be compelled from within their sin-cherishing souls to flee from God. His pure presence will bring to light their deep psychological reservoirs of guilt. They will feel within themselves an irrepressible impulse to run and hide, not because the divine face flashes with hostility, but because it shines brilliant with perfect love, which they have rejected and cannot bear to behold. God condemns all sin, precisely because He so fiercely loves all sinners, and the lost are now so identified with sin that they cannot help but feel condemnation in His holy presence. He loves them still, and He suffers infinite pain to lose them, for "God *is* love." He would save them if they would, if they *could*, embrace His love and turn from their sin, but they *will not* because they *cannot*, and they *cannot* because now they are void of the very capacity to know and love Him. Their sin-darkened hearts are forever blinded to the beauty of the divine character. Psychologically and emotionally they are left with only the capacity for feeling shame in His presence. Everything in them is urgent to flee from *The One* who was so good to them while they hated Him and lived for themselves to the hurt of others. Eternal love itself, by its very nature, is utter condemnation to sin and selfishness. It is by *contrast*, not by *sameness*, that God's presence is destructive to the wicked.

That's the first point regarding the second death—the wicked will encounter the unveiled face of God and experience all the self-awareness that the encounter will entail.

Second, as the wicked stand before God, Revelation 20 says, "there was found no place for them."

Wow!

No place for them at all, anywhere, in the new heavens and the new earth God is now establishing!

How tragic!

Those are perhaps the saddest words ever written, saddest of all for God—*"there was found no place for them."* The second death is total aloneness, complete separation from God, the source of life. As they stand before their Maker, the lost are flooded with a deep inner sense of complete unbelonging. Standing before God's throne and gazing upon His countenance, they realize with intense vividness that they are so out of harmony with His character that there is absolutely "no place for them." They don't fit into a universe governed by the voluntary rule of selfless love. They cannot exist among nor interact with a society of beings who live wholly for others. They can't even comprehend such a society, and to live there would be supreme torture to them. Sin has hollowed their hearts of the very capacity for love. Rebellion has stripped away the gentle emotional impulses of their hearts. Selfishness has eradicated the sensitive mental and emotional mechanisms of their humanity.

Third, as the wicked stand before God sensing that there is no place for them, record books are opened and they are judged by the things written in the books. This is the Bible's way of further describing the fact that the wicked will inevitably face the full reality of their sin and the guilt that accompanies it.

Sin, once committed, is an existing reality in the mind, in the *psyche*. It is on record in the conscience, and that record must either be resolved by God's forgiveness or come to light as the books are opened on the final day of reckoning. To bear ones own guilt on the Day of Judgment is the only alternative to a living faith-encounter with God's forgiveness. All human beings are sinners. The condemnation inherent in sin will ultimately impose an unbearable sense of self-loathing upon all who refuse to embrace the healing truth of God's pardoning grace. A conscious sense of God's love is the only power capable of neutralizing the destructive power of our guilt.

In order to grasp what the Bible means when it says, "the books were opened…and the dead were judged," try to imagine the unimaginable. Try to imagine what it would be like if you were made perfectly conscious of every sin you've ever committed:

Every self-serving thought, feeling, and action vivid in your mind!

Every ugly detail staring back at you in your conscience with nowhere to escape!

Then add to the horrendous picture an absolute absence of mercy.

No conception of forgiveness!

No sense of acceptance!

No idea of a God who freely and eagerly pardons all sin!

What would that moment in time be like for you? I know what it would be like for me:

Total psychological meltdown!

Complete mental implosion!

And it is this—precisely *this*—that the wicked will undergo as they stand before God and look into His eyes. The books will be opened, setting in motion an inescapable psychological replay within the realm of their conscience. Every hardened rebel will see the part he or she has played in the great war between good and evil and feel that weight of their own shame. Every deed of their lives will be exposed with crystal clarity. The blazing light of infinite love will clash in their minds against the dark ugliness of their sin.

Finally, as the wicked stand there reckoning with their guilt and lashing out with hatred against their Maker, Revelation 20 says that the wicked are destroyed in "the lake of fire." They do not live on endlessly in the flames. Earlier, in verse 9, John had already described the effect of this fire:

They went up on the breadth of the earth and surrounded the camp of the saints and the beloved city. And fire came down from God out of heaven and devoured them.

All of these factors—their encounter with the face of God, their realization that there is no place for them, the opening of the record books, and the fire that consumes their bodies—lead to the final, definitive statement in verse 14: *"This is the second death."*

Such will be the sad and final demise of all incorrigibly wicked human beings.

But here's the good news:

None need bear the psychological weight of their own sin and shame.

None need encounter God on the Day of Judgment with anything but sheer joy.

None need feel on that day that there is no place for them.

None need suffer the horrific reality of the second death.

Back in Revelation 20:6, a promise was made:

Blessed and holy is he who has part in the first resurrection. Over such the second death has no power.

This reminds us, of course, of the earlier promise we read in Revelation 2:14, which says that those who partake of the victory of Christ *"shall not be hurt by the second death."*

There is a profound gospel logic evident in these verses: if those who embrace the salvation of Jesus escape the *power* and *hurt* of *the second death*, Jesus must have suffered under its *power* for them and endured its *hurt* on their behalf.

And so He did.

We pick up the story in Matthew 26:36-38:

> Then Jesus came with them to a place called Gethsemane, and said to the disciples, "Sit here while I go and pray over there." And He took with Him Peter and the two sons of Zebedee, and He began to be sorrowful and deeply distressed. Then He said to them, "My soul is exceedingly sorrowful, even to death. Stay here and watch with Me."

A particular word should stand out to you here. When Jesus says, "My *soul* is exceedingly sorrowful, even to death," yes—you guessed it—He is using the same word He had previously employed to describe the second death:

Fear not them which kill the body, but are not able to kill the soul (psyche): *but rather fear Him which is able to destroy both soul* (psyche) *and body in hell.*

As He enters Gethsemane, Jesus is entering the dark psychological realm of our sin and shame. He is voluntarily venturing into hell on our behalf. He tells His disciples, *I am dying at the soul level of My being, at the psyche level.* It is crucial to notice that no physical abuse has yet been inflicted upon Jesus. He has not yet been whipped by the Roman soldiers. The crown of thorns has not been forced upon His head. The nails have not been driven through His hands and feet. And yet, in the absence of bodily torture, Jesus says He is dying. Right here, right now, in the quietude of a midnight garden, lethal forces are preying upon His *soul*. Make no mistake about it: Jesus is not dying a mere physical death from physical causes. He is experiencing the grim realities of the second death.

The account continues in verse 39:

> He went a little farther and fell on His face, and prayed, saying, "O My Father, if it is possible, let this cup pass from Me; nevertheless, not as I will, but as You will."

Throughout the Bible the symbolism of a full "cup" indicates that a person or a nation has reached the tipping point of its guilt, the point of no return, the point at which God must back up and allow them to suffer the consequences of their sins without His intervening mercy. In Gethsemane Jesus is beginning to lift this very cup to His lips. He is drinking, as it were, the full cup of human guilt into His own sinless, innocent psychological system. In 2 Corinthians 5:21 the apostle Paul describes the experience of Jesus with these startling words:

> For He (God the Father) made Him (Jesus) who knew no sin to be sin for us, that we might become the righteousness of God in Him.

Here is "the great exchange" of the gospel. Jesus, the sinless One, became sin for us, so that we might be become righteous through Him.

But how, in what concrete sense, did Jesus become sin for us?

Hundreds of years in advance, the prophet Isaiah graphically foretold precisely what Jesus would experience on our behalf. You will recall this Scripture from our message entitled, *The Savior.* Take in every line of Isaiah 53:6-12:

All we like sheep have gone astray;

We have turned, every one, to his own way;

And the Lord has laid on Him the iniquity of us all.

He was oppressed and He was afflicted, Yet He opened not His mouth; He was led as a lamb to the slaughter, And as a sheep before its shearers is silent, So He opened not His mouth.

He was taken from prison and from judgment, And who will declare His generation? For He was cut off from the land of the living; For the transgressions of My people He was stricken.

And they made His grave with the wicked—But with the rich at His death, Because He had done no violence, Nor was any deceit in His mouth.

Yet it pleased the Lord to bruise Him; He has put Him to grief. When You make His soul an offering for sin, He shall see His seed, He shall prolong His days, And the pleasure of the Lord shall prosper in His hand.

He shall see the labor of His soul, and be satisfied. By His knowledge My righteous Servant shall justify many, For He shall bear their iniquities.

Therefore I will divide Him a portion with the great, And He shall divide the spoil with the strong, Because He poured out His soul unto death, And He was numbered with the transgressors, And He bore the sin of many, And made intercession for the transgressors.

Four times the prophet emphasizes that Jesus will save fallen humanity by bearing their "transgressions," their "iniquities," their "sins." And three times Isaiah employs the word "soul" to describe the inner level at which the Savior would bear our sins:

- His *soul* will be made an offering for sin.
- By the labor of His *soul* He will achieve our salvation.
- He will pour out His *soul* unto death on our behalf.

More astounding words have never been written.

More astounding realities have never been set in motion.

And more astounding love has never been put on display.

According to Isaiah's prophecy, Jesus would become the sin bearer for the whole human race. He would literally give, pour out, and sacrifice the totality of Himself in order to secure our salvation.

On the one hand, there is the common physical death we all die, from which there is a resurrection. On the other hand, there is the ultimate death of both body and soul, which is the eternal death from which there is no resurrection. As Jesus entered Gethsemane He began to enter the dark realm of the second death. Apart from God's saving grace, sin imposes upon each person the excruciating psychological phenomenon the Bible calls *condemnation* or *guilt*. What we are now realizing is that Jesus did not merely experience the condemnation attached to one person's life of sin, but rather He bore "the iniquity of us all." He owned every evil motive and every wicked deed, every hateful feeling and every ugly thought, every rape and murder, every war and holocaust, every sin of every person. He owned it all. In His conscience He felt the tormenting blows of self-abhorrence that sin imposes as its ultimate exaction.

Clutching the cold ground in the garden of Gethsemane, three times Jesus prayed that agonized prayer:

> O My Father, if this cup cannot pass away from Me unless I drink it, Your will be done. (Matthew 26:42, 44)

Luke's Gospel informs us that at this point "an angel appeared to Him from heaven, strengthening Him." Then Luke explains why it was necessary for the angel to intervene. The internal agony pulsating in the mind of Christ was so intense that "His sweat was like great drops of blood falling down to the ground" (Luke 22:43-44).

Astounding!

The implication is clear: Jesus would have died in Gethsemane and never reached Calvary if the angel had not come to strengthen Him. And yet, the most intense suffering was yet to come.

Allow your imagination to see the final scenes as they are unfolded before us in Scripture.

The mob approaches and Jesus stands to meet them with regained composure, submitting Himself to the mob and asking that His disciples be set free.

Judas steps forward and places the kiss of betrayal upon that blood-stained cheek, and Jesus calls him "friend."

Peter lunges forward with his sword and takes off the ear of Malchus, the servant of the high priest. Jesus heals the wound and suppresses Peter's violent impulses.

Jesus tells Peter that He can, at will, call to His Father for twelve legions of angels to deliver Him, revealing that He is not trapped and that the sacrifice He is making is voluntary.

Jesus is arrested, illegally tried, repeatedly beaten, spit upon, mocked, and even abandoned and denied by His own disciples.

And then, with stripped down solemnity, Luke 23:33 brings us to the cross:

> And when they were come to the place, which is called Calvary, there they crucified Him.

The Roman soldiers drive nails through His hands and feet. Then the cross is lifted and dropped into the hole prepared for it. Every tendon of His body wrenches downward with the weight of His body. And yet, no word of complaint escapes His quivering lips. But it is not mere self-control that holds His tongue as they torture His body.

No!

We are rather witnessing the reality of a lesser pain eclipsed by a greater. What they're doing to His body recedes behind what's going on in His heart. The physical pain is horrible, no doubt, but it is superseded by the far greater agony of mind and heart He feels as He hangs there guilty on behalf of fallen humanity. Upon the cross, bearing the weight of the sin of the whole world, Jesus cries out, "My God, My God, why hast Thou forsaken Me?" (Matthew 27:46).

Hanging between heaven and earth, Jesus feels with acute sensitivity the separation that sin will ultimately make between God and unrepentant sinners. Now the eternal Son of the Father endures the horrific trauma of complete separation from His Father, separation from the One who has been His beloved companion for all eternity past. The feelings of guilt are so consuming that He feels utterly "forsaken," as if there is "no place for Him."

Here is the real sacrifice. And here is the apex revelation of divine love, because here we are face-to-face with the amazing truth that God literally loves fallen human beings more than His own existence. Jesus is now enveloped in a darkness of soul so impenetrable that He begins to feel that the separation between Himself and His Father will be eternal. The hopeful thoughts of His resurrection, concerning which He has recently spoken with such confidence, begin to fade from view.

Probing the depths of the ordeal, Psalm 88 peers into the internal workings of the mind of Christ as He hung upon the cross:

> O Lord, God of my salvation, I have cried out day and night before You. Let my prayer come before You; Incline Your ear to my cry.
>
> For my soul is full of troubles, And my life draws near to the grave. I am counted with those who go down to the pit; I am like a man who has no strength, Adrift among the dead, like the slain who lie in the grave, Whom You remember no more, And who are cut off from Your hand.
>
> You have laid me in the lowest pit, In darkness, in the depths. Your wrath lies heavy upon me, And You have afflicted me with all Your waves. Selah You have put away my acquaintances far from me; You have made me an abomination to them; I am shut up, and I cannot get out; My eye wastes away because of affliction.
>
> Lord, I have called daily upon You; I have stretched out my hands to You. Will You work wonders for the dead? Shall the dead arise and praise You? Selah. Shall Your loving kindness be declared in the grave? Or Your faithfulness in the place of destruction? Shall Your wonders be known in the dark? And Your righteousness in the land of forgetfulness?

As Jesus died on the cross, the mental and emotional darkness of our sin was so heavy upon Him that He felt as if He was sinking into a death from which there would be no resurrection. The entire prophecy is articulated in second death language:

- My soul is full of troubles
- Your wrath lies heavy upon me
- I am cut off from Your hand
- I am sinking into the lowest pit
- Into the place of destruction
- Into the land of forgetfulness
- I am shut up and I cannot get out
- Will You remember Me no more?
- Will I arise from the dead to praise you?

It is evident from this Messianic passage that Jesus faced the full horror of the second death on our behalf. Enveloped within the impenetrable darkness of our guilt, for a sustained period of time He could not see life for Himself beyond the grave. Crushed under the weight of our sin, the bright hope of resurrection eluded His grasp. And yet, faced with the bleak prospect of eternal separation from His Father, He still did not cease to choose our eternal life over His own.

As Jesus hangs between heaven and earth, reaching upward to His Father and downward to fallen humanity, there is an unspoken question that hangs heavy in the air, not only back then, but here and now: Does God love fallen human beings more than Himself? When faced with the ultimate decision to preserve Himself at the loss of others or to save others at the loss of Himself, what will God choose?

Jesus is the answer.

Deeper and deeper He sank into the dark pit of sin until the separation between Himself and His Father was complete, and until all the power and hurt of the second death were exhausted by His unrelenting love. In His final expiring prayer, He was victorious over sin and death: "Father, into Your hands I commit My spirit" (Luke 23:46). In these words Jesus entrusted His own eternal fate to the Father, hoping again for resurrection. Jesus died in faith, in hope, in love, and therefore in victory. "Through death" He ensured the destruction of "him who had the power of death, that is, the devil" (Hebrews 2:14). He "abolished death and brought life and immortality to light through the gospel" (2 Timothy 1:10).

By virtue of the fact that He died without yielding to sin, loving sinners with a perfect love void of all selfishness, death had no power to hold Him. Peter declared the truth of the matter in Acts 2:24:

> God raised Him from the dead, freeing Him from the agony of death, because it was impossible for death to keep its hold on Him. (NIV)

Why was it impossible for death to hold Him?

Because by selflessly loving us move than His own life, He conquered the power of Satan to claim the victory over Him! The Father did not resurrect Christ by arbitrary power, but by rightful conquest. He laid down His life for the salvation of the world, and by the power of that victory He arose to life again. And as He came forth from the grave, He had won eternal life for us all. Revelation 1:18:

> I am He who lives, and was dead, and behold, I am alive forevermore. Amen. And I have the keys of Hades and of Death.

And because He lives, all who put their trust in Him shall live also. So trust Him. In the light of His love for you, turn your heart to Him and live.

He didn't have to come to our rescue.

He didn't have to die on the cross as *The Sacrifice* for our sins.

He chose to.

And why?

For one simple and eternally profound reason: because He literally loves you and me more than His own life.

Only one question remains: Will you love Him in return?

If that is your desire, I invite you to slip to your knees as we pray.

Prayer and appeal.

Instructions on page 119

PRESENTER, PLEASE SHARE WITH YOUR AUDIENCE THAT THIS IS A SAFE ZONE.
It's a safe place to be themselves. • Everyone has the right to their own opinion.
There are no dumb questions. • All comments are encouraged and respected.

Discussion Questions

1. How does the idea of bodily death as unconscious sleep compare with what you have believed about death?

2. What is your reaction to this concept? Is it comforting? Upsetting? Difficult to accept? A relief?

3. Does it surprise you to learn that the Greek word for soul is *psyche*? What difference does this make, if any, to your ideas about souls and spirits?

4. What is your reaction to the concept of hell (the second death) as described in the Bible and in this message; that is, as eternal *death*, not as eternal life in torment?

5. How does it make you feel to think that a fully open, face-to-face encounter with God awaits you?

6. Do you agree that the reaction to this encounter would differ depending on your attitude toward and relationship with God? Why or why not?

7. What is your response to the story given of Jesus willingly choosing total separation from God so that you could gain total union with God?

THE MAKER

THE COMMUNICATOR

THE KING

THE SAVIOR

THE SPIRIT

THE GREAT GIVER

THE HEALER

THE SACRIFICE

THE NEW MAN

THE MESSENGER

THE BRIDEGROOM

THE BODY

09. THE NEW MAN
new life in Christ

BIBLE TEXT: I have been crucified with Christ; it is no longer I who live, but Christ lives in me; and the life which I now live in the flesh I live by faith in the Son of God, who loved me and gave Himself for me. (Galatians 2:20)

PRESENTER'S NOTE: Make an appeal in one of a few ways, according to the culture you are in or according to your personal reading of the composit personality and atmosphere of the crowd. Review the three different possible appeal approaches on page 145.

Prepare or buy cards ahead of time.

See pages 145, 146

the NEW MAN synopsis

Adam, the first man, could also be seen as the "old man." By his sin, he brought brokenness to all his descendants. But one Man, the New Man, Jesus, actualized a new life of perfect love and righteousness that now stands on record as a free gift to all human beings. God regards us as righteous even though we're not. He doesn't do this in order to excuse or perpetuate our sinful course of living, but rather to give us, as a gift, an entirely new identity of innocence and righteousness. We can choose active faith as the mechanism by which we become identified with Christ Jesus, *The New Man*, in order to assimilate His righteousness into our own lives. We can learn to live like who we are in Christ, not like who we are in ourselves.

The New Man

In this message we will spend our time exploring the astounding gospel truth that we, as fallen and sinful human beings, are offered an entirely new identity of innocence and righteousness in Jesus Christ.

Let's begin with a story.

Once there was a prostitute who met a man who knew her true worth.

Jenna had been in the business of selling herself since she was fourteen. Now she was in her twenty's, and putting a price tag on her body was all she knew. On this particular day, her pimp had dropped her off a few miles/kilometers from the city to make herself available by hitchhiking. After just a few moments with her thumb out, a car pulled over and the passenger door was flung open.

"I need a ride," she said to the man in the driver's seat, "but perhaps you need something too."

The middle-aged man just smiled and gestured with his hand for her to get in. As they drove along, the man asked the question she was expecting: "How much?"

"$100," Jenna nervously said, expecting, as usual, that he would try to talk her down.

To her surprise, the man said, "No, you are worth more than that."

"Oh, okay, how 'bout $150 then," she responded with a little excitement.

"No, no, you're worth more than that," he replied.

A little perplexed, but eager to make some fast money, Jenna stretched her mind to the highest amount she thought she was worth. "All right then, $500!"

Turning his eyes from the road, he looked straight into Jenna's eyes and said, "No way! Are you kidding?! You are worth far more than that."

Now Jenna was getting a little irritated. She had a hunch that this guy was just playing with her mind, and yet he seemed so polite and serious. So she went for the stars, half joking. "Why don't you take me on a world tour with no spending limit and give me a million dollars cash when it's all over," she laughed.

"No," he responded with a look of restrained emotion in his eyes. "You are far more valuable than that."

"Okay, Mister, you must be a gazillionaire."

"Not really, but I know value when I see it, and you are extremely valuable."

Now she had had enough. "WHAT DO WANT FROM ME?" she demanded.

"Just one thing. I'll give you all that I have and you'll never want for anything again. I'll supply all your needs. I only ask for one thing in exchange. Never sell yourself to any man ever again, and treat yourself like an innocent woman who has never sold herself."

"What! Don't you see what I am? I'm a prostitute. That's what I do and who I am."

"Yes, I see what you are. But I don't see a prostitute. I see a precious girl, a lovely lady, a beautiful person trapped in a life you really don't want to live. So I'm offering you a completely different life. A way out. A totally new identity."

You could say the man was just plain stupid, or you could say he was intelligent enough to see beyond her predicament to her potential.

You could call his offer an exercise in pretending, or you could call it a prophecy poised for fulfillment if she would simply believe his vision of her.

You could call his view of the woman blindness, or you could call it faith, a hope-imparting faith that might give her a whole new identity to live up to—his faith in her arousing her faith in him.

I'm happy to tell you that Jenna did accept the new identity offered to her. At first she felt like merely a rich prostitute. But after a while she began to feel like the daughter of an extremely kind man. Eventually she felt like she never was a prostitute at all. The old person she once was became a distant memory she could no longer relate to. The gracious faith of the good man transformed the woman. It was as if the old person she was had died, and now she was a completely new person, still the same Jenna she had always been but with all the bad stuff removed.

But this message really isn't about Jenna. It's about you and me.

The way the good man related to Jenna is precisely, in principle and practice, how God relates to all of us in order to achieve our salvation. He loves us with a love that looks beyond our sinfulness to our potential, and then He relates to us in such a way as to actualize that potential in our lives.

In order to build the picture, we'll look at a few passages from the writings of Paul, beginning with Romans 5:17-19:

> For if by the one man's offense death reigned through the one, much more those who receive abundance of grace and of the gift of righteousness will reign in life through the One, Jesus Christ. Therefore, as through one man's offense judgment came to all men, resulting in condemnation, even so through one Man's righteous act the free gift came to all men, resulting in justification of life. For as by one man's disobedience many were made sinners, so also by one Man's obedience many will be made righteous.

The idea here is so simple and beautiful. Adam sinned and brought condemnation "upon all men." His moral fall created a universal sin problem that has impacted all of us. Just look at all the evil and suffering in our world, as well as in your very own nature, and you get Paul's point. By natural birth we live in the legacy and aftermath of Adam. That's the bad news. But the good news is, inversely, as good as the bad news is bad. Actually, no, the good news far exceeds in goodness the badness of the bad news! Yes, Adam's legacy is tragic, even horrific. But God corrected Adam's failure by—get this—becoming a human being and living a righteous life of perfect love as a full-fledged member of the human race. In the historical person of Jesus Christ a whole new humanity was forged out of the old. A life of righteousness was actualized in Christ and now stands on record as a free gift to all human beings.

In Ephesians 2:15 Paul describes Jesus as the "New Man." In 1 Corinthians 15:45-47, he calls Jesus "the Last Adam" and the "Second Man." In other words, Jesus is a whole new representative human being—a recast prototype, if you will—containing in Himself a whole new set of realities that any and every human being may identify with and experience by faith.

He identified with us in order to elicit our identification with Him!

By His incarnation, Jesus entered into an intimate corporate solidarity with the human race and as such has become our new representative head. We need not continue to be who we are by natural birth, but may become sons and daughters of God by spiritual rebirth into the life of Christ. Our sinfulness and condemnation as children of Adam is our inherited reality, and if we choose to do so we can maintain that identity by continuing to identify with it. But there is another reality awaiting our consideration and apprehension, just as real but infinitely better. According to the gospel, there is a sense in which all that is true of us through Adam need not remain true of us if we will but choose, instead, to embrace the identity God has created for us in Christ, *The New Man.*

Earlier in the book of Romans, in chapter 4, verse 17, Paul explains the practical, relational dynamic God employs as He reaches out to us in Christ. He says that God, ". . . calls those things which do not exist as though they did."

In Paul's context he means that God regards us as righteous even though we're not. He doesn't do this in order to excuse or perpetuate our sinful course of living, but rather to give us, as a gift, an entirely new identity of innocence and righteousness. To condemn us as the spiritual prostitutes we are would only harden us in our sin and perpetuate the moral weakness our guilt imposes. God knows this. So He lifts the guilt from our hearts in order to place our feet on vantage ground. By relating to us as beautiful while we are yet morally ugly, He hopes to arouse in us a desire for moral beauty. By regarding us as righteous while we are yet sinners, He hopes to ignite in us the confidence needed to actually begin loving like He loves again. Because of the perfect righteousness that is achieved in Christ, God has faith in our potential to become righteous by His grace. His faith is so strong, in fact, that He "calls those things which do not exist as though they did."

In Romans chapter 6, the apostle Paul takes the next step in the logic of the gospel. Here he explains how we are called upon to identify with the gift of righteousness given to us in Christ. Let's take a look at verses 1-11:

> What shall we say then? Shall we continue in sin that grace may abound? Certainly not! How shall we who died to sin live any longer in it? Or do you not know that as many of us as were baptized into Christ Jesus were baptized into His death? There-fore we were buried with Him through baptism into death, that just as Christ was raised from the dead by the glory of the Father, even so we also should walk in new-ness of life. For if we have been united together in the likeness of His death, certainly

we also shall be in the likeness of His resurrection, knowing this, that our old man was crucified with Him, that the body of sin might be done away with, that we should no longer be slaves of sin. For he who has died has been freed from sin. Now if we died with Christ, we believe that we shall also live with Him, knowing that Christ, having been raised from the dead, dies no more. Death no longer has dominion over Him. For the death that He died, He died to sin once for all; but the life that He lives, He lives to God. Likewise you also, reckon yourselves to be dead indeed to sin, but alive to God in Christ Jesus our Lord.

There's a lot here, but we will simply highlight four key concepts:

1. When Jesus lived, died, was buried and then resurrected, Paul says we lived, died, were buried and resurrected in Him. Here, again, is Paul's corporate solidarity concept. Of course, individually and historically we were not participants in the Christ event. What Paul means is that Jesus did all that He did as our corporate representative, as the Second Adam.

2. Now then, Paul reasons, when each of us as individuals engage in the symbolic faith-act of baptism, we are identifying with the life, death, burial, and resurrection of Christ. The key idea behind baptism is identification with Christ, and by logical extension disassociation with what Paul here calls "the old man," which, in his context, is fallen Adam and all of us as his fallen posterity.

3. Paul then comes to his concluding point: since we have now identified with Christ by baptism, "we also should walk in newness of life," be "freed from sin," and "reckon" ourselves "to be dead indeed to sin, but alive to God in Christ Jesus our Lord."

4. To "reckon" means to *regard*, to *consider,* to *believe* something to be true. We are to reckon ourselves to be what we are not so that we may, by thus identifying ourselves, actually become that thing—namely, people who are alive to God and dead to sin, living in the crucified and resurrected life of Christ.

A physician does not become a physician by merely learning from books what a physician is. After all the book learning, he's still not truly a physician. But he must regard himself to be what he is not in order to become what he wants to be. He must *practice* medicine as one who has never practiced medicine in order to be a medical doctor. In the same way, we are not righteous, but God relates to us as righteous in order to instill in us the needed confidence to *practice* righteousness.

In other words, active faith is the mechanism by which we become identified with Christ Jesus, *The New Man,* in order to assimilate His righteousness into our own lives. In Galatians 2:20 Paul beautifully magnifies this idea in a single power-packed sentence:

> I have been crucified with Christ; it is no longer I who live, but Christ lives in me; and the life which I now live in the flesh I live by faith in the Son of God, who loved me and gave Himself for me.

When Jesus died on the cross, I died with Him. In one sense, I'm not alive anymore, but rather Christ is living in me. And yet, it is me, but now I'm living by faith in Him, moved in my new life of faith by the amazing reality of His love for me. As His life is lived out in me, my individuality is retained. It's Him living in me, but it's still me.

The salvation that Jesus has achieved on our behalf in Himself, and which He offers to each of us as our own personal experience, does not involve an eradication of our personal identities. Rather, it is a removal of those elements in us that are selfish and ugly while retaining and beautifying the natural traits of personality and character He has created us to possess. It's like combing out the unsightly tangles of a matted and knotted head of hair. It's still your hair, but now it's rearranged and smooth and beautiful. When Jesus saves you, you are still the unique you He created you to be. But He combs out the tangles and knots—the sin and guilt and pain—so that what remains is the beautiful you that you were always meant to be.

Paul continues in Romans 6:12-14:

> Therefore do not let sin reign in your mortal body, that you should obey it in its lusts. And do not present your members as instruments of unrighteousness to sin, but present yourselves to God as being alive from the dead, and your members as instruments of righteousness to God. For sin shall not have dominion over you, for you are not under law but under grace.

In other words, live like who you are in Christ, not like who you are in yourself. This is possible because you are not under the condemnation of the law as an unfaithful transgressor, but stand innocent under the grace of God by which He reckons you as righteous through the faithfulness of Jesus.

You may look at your life and see defeat, but in Christ you are more than a conqueror (Romans 8:37).

You may feel abandoned by God because of your failures, but in Christ you are an adopted child of God (Ephesians 1:5).

You may feel rejected and condemned for your sins, but you are "accepted in the Beloved," Christ Jesus (Ephesians 1:6).

You are all of this and so much more because He was all of this for you in the very same humanity you possess. He forged out an entirely new humanity of our old humanity. Entering into our very situation of weakness and defeat, He "condemned sin in the flesh" by refusing to yield to its power (Romans 8:3). He did this, not to pretend that we are something we are not, not to justify our sin, but to give us a new beginning point, so "that the righteousness of the law might be fulfilled in us, who walk not after the flesh, but after the Spirit" (Romans 8:4).

You could call God foolish for regarding us as righteous before we actually are, or you could call Him wise, wise enough to see beyond our predicament to our potential.

You could call His manner of relating to us mere pretending, or you could call it a self-fulfilling prophecy poised for fulfillment in all who believe.

You could call Him blind as He looks upon us as righteous in Christ, or you could understand that His faith has given us an entirely new identity to aspire toward.

But if you begin to believe, well, everything in your life would begin to change from the inside out. At first you'll feel like a wealthy prostitute. But soon you'll begin to feel like the child of an extremely kind heavenly Father. Eventually the old person that you once were will become merely a distant memory that you no longer relate to. The gracious faith of the rich Man—Christ who is rich in righteousness and love—will transform you into the beautiful new person He created you to be.

So then, the calling of the gospel is to become who you are in Christ, not to merely try harder to be a good person, not to ratchet up your willpower and "just do it," but to embrace, by faith, your true identity in Christ, *The New Man*. Then, from the vantage point of a new vision of yourself in Christ, moved to the core of your being by His self-sacrificing love for you, your life will be shaped and molded after His likeness.

In the light of all we've learned in this message, as well as in the previous messages of this series, I want to invite you to begin walking in newness of life with Christ. As we've learned, baptism is the biblically prescribed act of faith that signifies our initial identification with the righteous life, selfless death, and triumphant resurrection of Jesus Christ. After His resurrection, just prior to departing from our world, Jesus gave this amazing commission to all His followers in Matthew 28:18-20:

And Jesus came and spoke to them, saying, "All authority has been given to Me in heaven and on earth. Go therefore and make disciples of all the nations, baptizing them in the name of the Father and of the Son and of the Holy Spirit, teaching them to observe all things that I have commanded you; and lo, I am with you always, even to the end of the age." Amen.

As we close this message, I want to invite you to make a decision for Christ if you never have, to renew your commitment to Him if you have received Him in the past, and to be baptized as the tangible expression of your faith in Him.

> **Presenter:** *At this point you are going to make an appeal in one of a few ways, according to the culture you are in or according to your personal reading of the composite personality and atmosphere of the crowd. Following are three possible appeal approaches.*

- Appeal Number One—decision card

Right now, ushers are handing out a simple card.

> **Presenter:** *Make sure the cards are handed out quickly and smoothly. The ushers should be as close to invisible as possible. Prepare them ahead of time to simply walk up the aisles at a steady pace, handing out prepared stacks of cards to the first person in each aisle.*

Prepare or purchase cards ahead of time

Please put your name and contact information on the card, and put a check or X on the lines that apply to you.

1. ____I believe in Jesus and choose to accept Him as my personal Savior.

2 ____I want to be baptized to signify my faith in Christ.

3 ____I want to talk with someone about being baptized.

The ushers will now collect the cards as you turn them over and pass them to the center aisle as _____ sing a beautiful song titled _____.

> **Presenter:** *After the song, have prayer.*

- **Appeal Number Two—altar call**

First, I want to appeal to you to receive Jesus Christ as your personal Savior. If you've never made this decision, right now is a great time do so as we find our hearts moved by His great love for us.

Secondly, I want to invite you to signify your faith in Christ by being baptized—or re-baptized if you have lost your connection with Christ or if you were merely baptized in the past as a matter of religious formality.

Thirdly, if you are not sure about baptism but would like to explore the possibility, I appeal to you as well to move forward with that exploration.

As_____ sings a beautiful song titled_____, come forward if any of these three appeals applies to you.

> **Presenter:** Once the song ends, offer prayer.

I praise God for the decision each of you has made. Please bow your heads as we pray.

- **Appeal Number Three—raised hand**

> **Presenter:** Use the same three part appeal as in Appeal Number Two, but begin by asking them to bow their head for prayer, and then ask for raised hands at the end of each of the three appeals. Then, when your prayer ends, ask that those who raised their hands remain after and meet at the front as people depart. Once they gather, lead them into whatever plans you have for further connection with the pastor or elders or Bible workers in order to facilitate following through with their decision.

PRESENTER, PLEASE SHARE WITH YOUR AUDIENCE THAT THIS IS A SAFE ZONE.
It's a safe place to be themselves. • Everyone has the right to their own opinion.
There are no dumb questions. • All comments are encouraged and respected.

Discussion Questions

1. What did you think of the opening story of Jenna, who thought she was only a prostitute? Have you experienced this offer of new life and identity? Would you like to?

2. Discuss in your group how you think Jenna's new identity would play out. What are some of the steps she might go through on her way to full acceptance? During that time, is she really "new" or not?

3. Can you think of any other way God could have saved us?

4. What is the difference between trying to change by changing behavior and being changed from the inside out—attitudes first, actions afterward?

5. In what ways have you or have you not lived the truth of being crucified and resurrected with Christ? What would you like to change or stretch?

6. What do you think is meant by "active faith"? Is there such a thing as inactive faith? Why or why not?

7. Along the lines of the example of messy hair being combed out smooth and beautiful, try to describe the person you would be if this were becoming true in your life. What is preventing it from being so?

THE MAKER

THE COMMUNICATOR

THE KING

THE SAVIOR

THE SPIRIT

THE GREAT GIVER

THE HEALER

THE SACRIFICE

THE NEW MAN

THE MESSENGER

THE BRIDEGROOM

THE BODY

10. THE MESSENGER
new life in Christ

BIBLE TEXT: Then I saw another angel flying in the midst of heaven, having he everlasting gospel to preach to those who dwell on the earth—to every nation, tribe, tongue, and people—saying with a loud voice, "Fear God and give glory to Him, for the hour of His judgment has come; and worship Him who made heaven and earth, the sea and springs of water." (Revelation 14:6, 7)

PRESENTER'S NOTE:

- Read. Read. Read.
- Let this message soak into your mind.
- Take the time to make it your own.

  Review all the discussion questions early.

the MESSENGER synopsis

We are made in the image of God, and created to communicate and connect with Him and with each other. God is the great communicator; in fact, Jesus is called the Word. He not only preached the message, He *is* the Message—the good news of the gospel. We will examine the context, content, and consummation of the gospel as given in one particular passage in Revelation. The *content* is the long battle of the dragon, the devil, against the woman, God's church. The *content* is three angels reminding the earth of the Everlasting Gospel and warning the nations to return to worship of the one true God, as the end, and therefore the judgment, is near. The *consummation* is the glorious Second Coming and a new beginning for all things, forever!

The Messenger

In 1981, during a solo crossing of the Atlantic Ocean, Steven Callahan's 21-foot (6.5 meter) self-built sailboat, *Napoleon Solo*, hit a whale during a storm and sank. Callahan managed to escape with limited survival gear into his life raft. Little did he know, that small life raft would be his home as he floated slowly toward the Caribbean for 76 days! His courageous survival is half ingenuity and seamanship and half miracle. His 76-days spent adrift and lost at sea is the longest a single person has ever endured. During the journey, at various times, Callahan would write messages to friends and family, place them in small bottles, and throw them out to sea. He was longing to communicate, to be heard.

It is a most natural longing, the longing to communicate. Being deprived of all social interaction for such a lengthy period of time is neither natural nor easy. Futile though it seemed, Callahan felt the deep need to communicate, to send a message to his loved ones.

A Beautiful God and a Beautiful Message

As we have learned in this series, mankind is made in the image of God. As such, we were made to communicate and to connect. God is revealed in Scripture as a communicator. In fact, the very first act attributed to God in the Bible is the act of creation *by speaking*. "Then God said, 'Let there be light'; and there was light" (Genesis 1:3). The phrase, "Then God said" appears eight times in Genesis chapter one, and the phrase, "Thus says the Lord" occurs nearly 500 times in the Old Testament; it is, in fact, one of the best known and most frequently and widely used phrases in the entire Bible.

The point cannot be missed: God is a communicator.

This makes perfect sense with what we've been learning about God in this series. "God is love" (1 John 4:8) is a truth that we keep coming back to over and over again. The character and nature of God is so beautiful and awesome—it's such good news!—that it's been our main building block from the beginning of this series.

Love cannot be kept to itself. It must communicate. It must be communicated. It is its nature to do so. Love flows out to *others*; it longs to reach and connect. Steven Callahan in his oceanic isolation longed for social connection and contact; he longed to communicate. Of course he did! We all do! It's part of what it means to be made in the image of God, to be human.

150

In prisons, one of the most trying and tortuous punishments that can be inflicted is what's called "solitary confinement." It means just what it sounds like: being alone. Why, though, is it so trying and difficult? Simple—as social beings, we long to connect and communicate, just like God.

We've mentioned it before, but it bears repeating that it's no wonder that Jesus Christ is actually called "The Word" in Scripture (John 1:1). What an amazing revelation! The purpose of words is to communicate. Communicate what? Well, what else? The thoughts and feelings of the speaker! Jesus Christ, then, was not only a messenger; He was Himself *the message*—God's message to a dying and dark planet.

The Bible calls this message the gospel. Yes, Jesus *is* the gospel! He not only preached the gospel, He *was* the gospel. His life, death, and resurrection were God's message to us all, and this story, this holy history of Jesus Christ is the gospel, the good news. Actually, that's what the word gospel means: good news.

So Jesus is Himself the good news. This is exactly the Apostle Paul's point in 1 Corinthians 15:1-5,

> Moreover, brethren, I declare to you the gospel which I preached to you, which also you received and in which you stand, by which also you are saved, if you hold fast that word which I preached to you—unless you believed in vain. For I delivered to you first of all that which I also received: that Christ died for our sins according to the Scriptures, and that He was buried, and that He rose again the third day according to the Scriptures, and that He was seen by Cephas, then by the twelve.

Give information about the series on Revelation and Prophecy coming up.

Did you catch that? Paul's very definition of the gospel is the life, death, and resurrection of Jesus Christ. So, again, Jesus not only preached the good news, He *was* the good news. He not only spoke the word, He *was* the word—both the Messenger and the Message!

He was God's message of love, God's love letter if you will, to you and to me and everyone. Jesus came to show us what kind of a person God is. This is what He meant when He said things like, "He who has seen Me has seen the Father" (John 14:9).

And Paul said things like, "For in Him dwells all the fullness of the Godhead bodily" (Colossians 2:9). That is, everything that God is in His person and character was revealed to us in the holy history, the message, of Jesus Christ.

Talk about a beautiful picture of God! That picture has been unfolding grandly, gloriously, and graciously right before our very eyes. We have seen that Jesus truly is The One. His character as The Maker, The King, The Savior, The Healer, and more is a thing of beauty to behold. But it is even more than a beautiful thing to merely behold; He is a beautiful person to be known, to be loved, and to be loved *by*.

A Timely Message

In this series we've not spent a lot of time in the book of Revelation, though it is one of the most interesting and mysterious books in the entire Bible. There is a follow-up series to this one that spends quite a bit of time in the book of Revelation. If you have an interest in that—which surely you do, right?—then you'll want to be sure to attend that series. Now, while we haven't spent too much time in Revelation up to this point, we're going to spend the rest of our time in this presentation seeking to understand one particular passage, a passage that revolves around a timely and important message. In fact, it's three messages that together make up the whole message.

The passage is found in Revelation 14:6-12. Some of the language and images may be a little new or seemingly strange, but don't worry. We're not going to be able to address every detail of this critically important three-part message, but we are going to understand the main thrust and grasp of just *why* it's such an important and timely message. We'll look at the message in three parts:

1. The Context of the Message

2. The Content of the Message

3. The Consummation of the Message

You ready? Alright! Here we go...

The Context of the Message

Before getting into the message itself, let's see *where* this message occurs in the chronology of Revelation. Revelation 12 and 13 depict a terrible Satanic attack against God's people. We've learned about this war in several of our earlier presentations, especially our third message, *The King*.

Satan, God's enemy, is referred to in Revelation as a "dragon" (Revelation 12:9). He is depicted as waging a war against God Himself in the very courts of heaven (v. 7). This war is not primarily a physical battle, but a battle of ideas. You will recall that it's a war over God's character and government. In the course of this ongoing conflict, Satan and his angelic sympathizers are "cast out" of heaven (v. 9). Undeterred, they then turn their attention to human beings, God's own children. And what better way is there to hurt a father than to hurt or threaten His children?

Satan works not so much by power, as by subtlety and deceit. He overcame Adam and Eve and turned their loyalty and affection away from their Creator and Father. Revelation 12 says that Satan "persecuted the woman" (v. 13). This woman is the people of God, the church. Since the time of Adam and Eve to the present, Satan, God's sworn enemy, has been waging a tireless war against the human race, which is really a war against God Himself.

This war will not continue forever, however. It will come to an end, and Revelation 13 and 14 tell that story.

Revelation 13 is a chapter that we'll take up in much greater detail in our next series of presentations. It is an important but admittedly mysterious and heavily symbolic chapter. Even so, the basic picture is easily grasped: as this lengthy conflict is drawing toward its close, Satan employs two terrible "beasts" to his advantage. These are not literal beasts, but kingdoms, nations; they are symbolic. It is not our point here to identify either of these two beasts, but to notice that they are Satan's final, desperate attack against the people of God.

The last verse of Revelation 12 says these haunting words: "And the dragon was enraged with the woman, and he went to make war with the rest of her offspring, who keep the commandments of God and have the testimony of Jesus Christ" (v. 17). Clearly, this is all out war at this point.

Revelation 13 then tells us *how* the dragon will carry out this final onslaught against God and His people: he uses two horrific beasts. One rises from the sea, the other from the earth. Here's John's picturesque and highly symbolic account of what he saw when he first laid eyes on the sea-beast:

> Then I stood on the sand of the sea. And I saw a beast rising up out of the sea, having seven heads and ten horns, and on his horns ten crowns, and on his heads a blasphemous name. Now the beast which I saw was like a leopard, his feet were like the feet of a bear, and his mouth like the mouth of a lion.

> The dragon gave him his power, his throne, and great authority. And I saw one of his heads as if it had been mortally wounded, and his deadly wound was healed. And all the world marveled and followed the beast. So they worshiped the dragon who gave authority to the beast; and they worshiped the beast, saying, "Who is like the beast? Who is able to make war with him?"... It was granted to him to make war with the saints and to overcome them. And authority was given him over every tribe, tongue, and nation. (Revelation 13:1-4, 7)

Talk about a wild-looking animal!

John then saw the second beast:

> Then I saw another beast coming up out of the earth, and he had two horns like a lamb and spoke like a dragon. And he exercises all the authority of the first beast in his presence, and causes the earth and those who dwell in it to worship the first beast, whose deadly wound was healed. He performs great signs, so that he even makes fire come down from heaven on the earth in the sight of men. And he deceives those who dwell on the earth by those signs which he was granted to do in the sight of the beast, telling those who dwell on the earth to make an image to the beast who was wounded by the sword and lived. (Revelation 13:11-14)

This second beast, which rises from the earth as opposed to the sea, is a most unusual beast as well. What makes this beast unique and particularly dangerous is that it possesses the characteristics of both a "dragon" and a "lamb." Jesus, of course, is "the Lamb of God who takes away the sin of the world" (John 1:29); the "dragon" is, as we've already seen, none other than Satan, God's sworn enemy. So this beast—a nation or kingdom—has attributes of both the devil and the Savior. Talk about an unusual and unexpected mixture!

Now recall that our purpose at this point is not to identify either of these highly symbolic beasts, but to note where they fit in the larger picture of Revelation, chapters 12-14.

To review, chapter 12 paints the picture of a "war in heaven." It ends with a declaration of all out, no-holds-barred war declared by Satan against God's people. Then comes chapter 13 in which John was shown the *means* by which this war would be conducted: two terrible, deceitful, and frightening beasts which, as we'll see in our next series, represent nations. These two beasts and their confederacy are so overwhelmingly powerful that the people, according to John, actually cry out: "Who is like the beast? Who is able to make war with him?" (Revelation 13:4). The answer is seemingly *no one*!

But then Revelation 14 comes, and here's where we find the very three-part message that we're seeking to understand in this presentation. This chapter can be divided easily into three parts:

1. A vision of those who are, in fact, victorious over the beastly confederacy
2. The message that enables them to be victorious
3. A picture of the ultimate result of that amazing message: the Second Coming of Jesus Christ

Those who are victorious are seen by John as "standing on Mount Zion" (Revelation 14:1). They are 144,000 in number and are standing with—who else? The Lamb, Jesus Christ! John wants the reader to know with certainty that the beastly confederacy will not prevail and that Jesus and His followers will be ultimately victorious. Ultimate victory had already been announced back in Revelation 12:11: "And they overcame him by the blood of the Lamb and by the word of their testimony, and they did not love their lives to the death."

John's point is that though it will *look* like an end-time beastly confederacy will be unstoppable and will ultimately destroy God's people, and thus His saving plan, that attack will fail and God's message, plan, and people will be victorious! Talk about good news!

So what about that three-part message in verses 6-12? It must be a powerful message to accomplish what it does in the face of such seemingly overwhelming odds.

It is to this amazing message that we now turn our attention.

The Content of the Message

The message, as we've said before, consists of three parts. Each part is delivered by an angel, thus there are three angels. This is why we're calling this message the "Three Angels' Message."

First, what's an angel anyway? Probably, you've got some mental picture of what an angel is. You know, white, wings, clouds, harps. Really, though, an angel is a messenger! In fact, that's what the word actually means—messenger. Think, for example, of the word *evangelist*. What is an evangelist? Easy! One who carries a message, usually, though not always, a religious one. Now if we take the "ev" off the beginning and the "ist" off the end, what root word are we left with? Angel!

This is our point exactly! An angel is a messenger.

Let's now read through this three-part message. Now remember, this is the very message that results in the Second Coming and gives the people of God full and final victory over Satan's last desperate attack. So this is super important stuff and deserves our careful and thoughtful attention.

Here it is, verses 6-12:

> Then I saw another angel flying in the midst of heaven, having the everlasting gospel to preach to those who dwell on the earth—to every nation, tribe, tongue, and people—saying with a loud voice, "Fear God and give glory to Him, for the hour of His judgment has come; and worship Him who made heaven and earth, the sea and springs of water." And another angel followed, saying, "Babylon is fallen, is fallen, that great city, because she has made all nations drink of the wine of the wrath of her fornication." Then a third angel followed them, saying with a loud voice, "If anyone worships the beast and his image, and receives his mark on his forehead or on his hand, he himself shall also drink of the wine of the wrath of God, which is poured out full strength into the cup of His indignation. He shall be tormented with fire and brimstone in the presence of the holy angels and in the presence of the Lamb. And the smoke of their torment ascends forever and ever; and they have no rest day or night, who worship the beast and his image, and whoever receives the mark of his name." Here is the patience of the saints; here are those who keep the commandments of God and the faith of Jesus.

> There's definitely a great deal of good stuff here that demands our attention. We won't have time to go into every detail and nuance of the whole message, but we are going to seek to understand it as best we can, since, again, this is the message that brings full and final victory over Satan and his plans.

The First Angel

> Then I saw another angel flying in the midst of heaven, having the everlasting gospel to preach to those who dwell on the earth—to every nation, tribe, tongue, and people—saying with a loud voice, "Fear God and give glory to Him, for the hour of His judgment has come; and worship Him who made heaven and earth, the sea and springs of water" (verses 6 and 7).

Several things jump out at us here.

First, the very first thing we're told about the angel is that he has "the everlasting gospel!" Praise God! We know what that is because it's what we opened this presentation with: the gospel is the good news of the holy history of Jesus Christ—His life, death, and resurrection! No wonder this message is so powerful, it's bathed in the good news of Jesus Christ and His loving salvation! In fact, that's what all of the rest of the message is really about: the gospel.

Notice now that this good news message is for everyone. Yes, everyone! The angel says, "every nation, tribe, tongue, and people." That's the Bible's way of saying that this is a universal message that every person needs to hear. What a beautiful and loving God indeed. He doesn't favor certain peoples, nations, colors, or ethnicities. He wants His message of salvation to be heard by the whole world! What's the best-known verse in all the Bible? John 3:16, "For God so loved the world that He gave His only begotten Son, that whoever believes in Him should not perish but have everlasting life." Don't forget that: He loves the *whole* world. Like the old children's song says, "red and yellow, black and white, all are precious in His sight."

The next part of the message, in verse 7, invites us to "fear God and give glory to him." Now don't be tempted to misunderstand this. The fear spoken of here is not a terror or fright that you would feel toward someone who meant you harm. No, no. This fear is a deep reverence and respect for the Being and Person that God is. He is, after all, God! And that makes Him really powerful and really awesome. But the good news is that, well, He's good!

The call, then, is to recognize and respect God's majesty and might, and to live our life in such a way that it gives Him the honor and "glory" He deserves. God could, with His power, compel our obedience and reverence, but He most certainly does not. He invites it and desires it, but leaves us free to serve, honor, and worship—or not. This is actually the very reason that He deserves our honor and praise, because He could demand it by His strength, but instead He invites it by His goodness and love. Beautiful!

The angel then speaks of "judgment," saying that the "hour has come." Here again, we'd be tempted to misunderstand this, but definitely shouldn't. Judgment, according to the Bible, isn't the bad news that many might believe. Quite the opposite, actually. Judgment is actually good news, since God's judgment is always fair, just, and equitable. And since believers are trusting Jesus as both their judge (John 5:22) and their lawyer and advocate (1John 2:1), judgment is always given, in the words of Daniel the prophet, who wrote about the judgment, "in favor of the saints" (Daniel 7:22). That is, God's judgment always comes down favorably on those who trust Jesus Christ and who believe the gospel!

We'll talk more about the timing and details of this judgment in our next series. It's a fascinating and important subject, but not one that should cause you terror or anxiety. Its job, in part, is to teach us to look to and trust Jesus Christ more fully.

What does the first angel close with? Creation! In a sense, he *ends* with the *beginning*. "In the beginning, God created the heavens and the earth," is the timeless opening line of Scripture. This is what our very first lesson, *The Maker*, addressed. After all, if God is our Creator, it's the very best place to start, since it's the place that we, as human beings, started. No wonder that's where the Bible itself starts!

This is a very special call, and one not to be missed. The angel invites us to worship God as the Creator, "Him who made heaven and earth, the sea and springs of water." Well, how does someone do that? They keep God's memorial of creation, of course; they keep the Sabbath! This is familiar ground for us, since we spent an entire lesson on it. We learned in that lesson that the Sabbath is a sign of God's tremendous and incomparable love, both *creating* love and *redeeming* love.

The Sabbath, sadly, has been neglected and lost sight of in these busy, hustle and bustle, modern times, but the first angel assures us that it will come back to prominence in a global and beautiful way, bathed in the good news of the "everlasting gospel."

This, though, raises a question. How and when and why was the Sabbath lost sight of? This is a critically important question that we'll take up with great enthusiasm and detail in our next series. For now, though, we can say that the Sabbath became clouded by the traditions of men and a compromising church. Its history is a fascinating and tragic one. But, according to the first angel, that history doesn't end on a bad note. Oh no! The Sabbath, and the creation and redemption is memorializes, will be made front and center, on a global scale, as part of the message that finally defeats Satan's deceptive and coercive attacks.

So there you have it. The first angel's message is rooted in the good news of the "everlasting Gospel," the respect and reverence that God rightly deserves, the good news that Jesus is our judge, and the invitation to worship God as our Creator by keeping His seventh-day Sabbath.

Now, what about that second angel?

The Second Angel

> And another angel followed, saying, "Babylon is fallen, is fallen, that great city, because she has made all nations drink of the wine of the wrath of her fornication". (verse 8)

Whoa, talk about some interesting and picturesque language!

This message is unmistakably clear. It announces the certain fall of end-time Babylon. This, though, raises the obvious question: *what is* end-time Babylon? The short answer is that it is a fallen and failed religious system. Yes, you heard that right: Babylon is a religious system, fallen because of its false teachings and its illegitimate relations with "the kings of the earth."

Here's how John describes Babylon later in Revelation:

> Then one of the seven angels who had the seven bowls came and talked with me, saying to me, "Come, I will show you the judgment of the great harlot who sits on many waters, with whom the kings of the earth committed fornication, and the inhabitants of the earth were made drunk with the wine of her fornication." So he carried me away in the Spirit into the wilderness. And I saw a woman sitting on a scarlet beast which was full of names of blasphemy, having seven heads and ten horns. The woman was arrayed in purple and scarlet, and adorned with gold and precious stones and pearls, having in her hand a golden cup full of abominations and the filthiness of her fornication. And on her forehead a name was written: MYSTERY, BABYLON THE GREAT, THE MOTHER OF HARLOTS AND OF THE ABOMINATIONS OF THE EARTH. I saw the woman, drunk with the blood of the saints and with the blood of the martyrs of Jesus. And when I saw her, I marveled with great amazement. (Revelation 17:1-6)

Wow! Even more picturesque and highly symbolic imagery. And yet even if you don't grasp the meaning of all of the symbols and context, the basic picture is still quite clear: a fallen, harlot-like woman is riding a beast and making war with God's people. In both the Old and the New Testaments, the people of God, whether Israel or the Church, are often referred to as a woman. (See, for example, Jeremiah 6:2; Ezekiel 16; 2 Corinthians 11:2; and 2 John 1:13.) As we've already mentioned, these symbolic prophetic beasts represent nations or kingdoms.

So put the pieces together and what do we have here? A fallen and unfaithful church in command of a beastly and terrifying nation. In short: a terrible, destructive, and persecuting end-time union of church and state. This is not a pretty picture. And, in fact, the history of the church down through the ages hasn't always been a pretty picture. This is a sad but true fact that the church has to own up to. The church, especially during the medieval period, also called the Dark Ages, was regularly caught up in inappropriate relations with the state. It's a tragic and terrible history.

That history, though, according to John in Revelation, is going to be repeated, but on an even larger scale. In fact, a *global* scale!

The good news, though, is that the second angel announces the downfall of this terrible, tragic, and coercive church-state union! The message that brings it down is—what else? The gospel of Jesus Christ.

We'll go into greater detail about this end-time Babylon in our next series, which addresses more prophetic and end-time topics. Be on the lookout for that! It's going to be great!

And, finally, the third angel...

The Third Angel

> Then a third angel followed them, saying with a loud voice, "If anyone worships the beast and his image, and receives his mark on his forehead or on his hand, he himself shall also drink of the wine of the wrath of God, which is poured out full strength into the cup of His indignation. He shall be tormented with fire and brimstone in the presence of the holy angels and in the presence of the Lamb. And the smoke of their torment ascends forever and ever; and they have no rest day or night, who worship the beast and his image, and whoever receives the mark of his name." Here is the patience of the saints; here are those who keep the commandments of God and the faith of Jesus. (verses 9-12)

This is, admittedly, the toughest part of the message to understand. It revolves around so many end-time symbols and issues, not the least of which is the mysterious "mark of the beast." This being the case, we're going to leave nearly all of this part of the message to our next series which, again, will address these prophetic images and scenarios.

There is, though, one thing that we have to understand, and fortunately it's very easily grasped: God's last-day, victorious people will have the perfect harmony of both keeping God's commandments and trusting totally in the saving faithfulness of Jesus Christ. It's not one or the other, but both since Jesus is *both* Savior *and* King! In fact, we had two presentations by those very names: *The Savior* and *The King*.

We already know that we don't obey the King's good rules and commandments *in order to be saved*, but because by trusting in Jesus Christ, the Savior, *we already are saved!*

These end-time people who are victorious over the dragon, and who endure to the end, are in possession of the perfect balance of obedience and faith. They don't emphasize one at the expense of the other, but hold to the essential beauty and significance of both: one as the *root*, the other as the *fruit*.

So there you have it! Talk about a powerful three-part message! Truly, "What then shall we say to these things? If God is for us, who can be against us?" (Romans 8:31). This message is the very message that will prevail over God's enemy, Satan, in the final conflict. It is a message that we've just scratched the surface of here, but it is a message that deserves our serious attention.

This is a message that centers on Him who is the Message, Jesus Christ! He is "King of Kings and Lord of Lords," and "He shall reign forever and ever" (Revelation 19:16; Revelation 11:15).

This picture of Jesus victorious turns our minds naturally to the third part of our presentation...

The Consummation of the Message

Look what happens as the *result* of the world-wide proclamation and exposure of the Three Angels' Messages:

> Then I looked, and behold, a white cloud, and on the cloud sat One like the Son of Man, having on His head a golden crown, and in His hand a sharp sickle. And another angel came out of the temple, crying with a loud voice to Him who sat on the cloud, "Thrust in Your sickle and reap, for the time has come for You to reap, for the harvest of the earth is ripe." So He who sat on the cloud thrust in His sickle on the earth, and the earth was reaped (Revelation 14:14-16).

Here again, as with nearly everything in the book of Revelation, the language is highly symbolic. But the symbolism here cannot be missed, since it draws on the very language and imagery of much of the rest of Scripture: the imagery of the harvest.

The harvest was, and is, a time of joy, completion, and satisfaction. The ground has been worked, the seed has been sown, the crop has been tended to and has grown. And now, finally, the harvest comes!

Jesus is here depicted, like a farmer, as reaping the earth. What is He reaping? Corn? Wheat? Beans? No! He's reaping His people, His beloved people. The conflict is closing, the victory is won, and Jesus comes to rescue and reap His children. This great truth of the Second Coming is so important and beautifully relational, our whole next presentation is about it! It's called *The Bridegroom*, and it's our second-to-last part of this series. Wow, we've come a long way, haven't we? But the journey, of course, is just beginning.

Now don't miss the huge significance of what we've covered here and learned in this presentation! Here it is, in brief: *The Three Angels' Message is the very message that precedes the Second Coming of Jesus Christ to earth!*

That makes this a very, very important message! And indeed we have found it to be so. What is the essence of the message? Here are the parts we've seen thus far:

1. The everlasting Gospel of Jesus Christ

2. The global scope of the message and God's love for everyone, regardless of race, nation, or language

3. The call to revere God and to live our life to glorify and honor Him

4. The call to worship God as our Creator

5. The demise of all fallen and false religious systems

6. The end-time believers' perfect balance of faith and obedience

7. The endurance of the believers, which consummates in the Second Coming of Christ

Talk about a truly powerful, truly life-changing message! It's a message about the One—*The One!*—who is Himself the Message.

It's a message worth hearing and telling! There's no more important message in all the world.

Well, you've heard it! Won't you join me and millions of others in telling it?

PRESENTER, PLEASE SHARE WITH YOUR AUDIENCE THAT THIS IS A SAFE ZONE.
It's a safe place to be themselves. • Everyone has the right to their own opinion.
There are no dumb questions. • All comments are encouraged and respected.

Discussion Questions

1. Have you ever been completely alone for an extended time? How did it feel?

2. How do you think it would feel to be unable to contact your loved ones for a long time? Do you think God feels that way about some of us?

3. What do you think it means that Jesus is "the Word"?

4. Briefly share what you knew or were taught about the book of Revelation before this presentation.

5. Did you ever think of Revelation being about the Everlasting Gospel? What is your reaction to this idea?

6. How much did you understand about the context of the battle between the dragon and the woman? Discuss briefly, and decide if you are interested in a later presentation of more about this book of the Bible.

7. What do you think of the content of the messages brought by the three angels? Is it comforting? Frightening? Both?

8. Can you see the connection of the seventh day Sabbath? Have you been keeping it? If not, are you ready to try it?

9. Can you see the joy of this message? What impact do you think it will have on your life?

THE MAKER

THE COMMUNICATOR

THE KING

THE SAVIOR

THE SPIRIT

THE GREAT GIVER

THE HEALER

THE SACRIFICE

THE NEW MAN

THE MESSENGER

THE BRIDEGROOM

THE BODY

11. THE BRIDEGROOM

the second coming

BIBLE TEXT: Let not your heart be troubled; you believe in God, believe also in Me. In My Father's house are many mansions; if it were not so, I would have told you. I go to prepare a place for you. And if I go and prepare a place for you, I will come again and receive you to Myself; that where I am, there you may be also. (John 14:1-3)

PRESENTER'S NOTE: Prepare the list on page 169 to show via PowerPoint or on a board.

the **BRIDEGROOM** synopsis

This message examines the topic of Jesus' Second Coming from three viewpoints: Why is Jesus coming? (Because He loves us passionately and can't wait to live with us forever!) When will He come? (The Bible lists many negative signs by which we will know the coming is soon. It also lists a positive sign—one we have some control over!) How will He come? (The way He went—visibly, personally, and tangibly.) The Advent will be wonderful if one has chosen to follow God and His Way of Love, terrifying if one has chosen otherwise. Those who go with Christ will see, hear, touch, and live with Him forever in unimaginable glory.

The Bridegroom

It is a universal truism that those who are in love cannot bear to be separated. Lover and beloved must find the fastest way to be together, and until that day comes there is a distinct longing hovering over their lonely hearts. They watch time tick by with an ever-present consciousness of the space between them.

Anyone who's ever been in love knows this to be true.

What many don't know is that this is the underlying truth that informs the biblical subject of Christ's Second Coming.

We will unpack the topic in three parts:

Why is Jesus coming?

When will Jesus come?

How will Jesus come?

Why is Jesus Coming?

The short answer to the question is simply this: Jesus is coming again because He loves you and wants to be with you. But now let's expand the answer.

In John's Gospel, as Jesus begins His public ministry, John the Baptist identifies Christ with a very fascinating and enlightening title. Those who had been following John were kind of bothered by the fact that lots of people were beginning to follow Jesus instead of John. In John 3:29-30 we read the Baptist's response to their concern:

> He who has the bride is the bridegroom; but the friend of the bridegroom, who stands and hears Him, rejoices greatly because of the bridegroom's voice. Therefore this joy of mine is fulfilled. [30] He must increase, but I must decrease.

John sees in Jesus the heavenly bridegroom who has come to our world to claim His bride, and he sees himself as merely the friend, or what we would call the best man, of the groom.

It is perfectly acceptable and right, John explains, that the people should be attracted to Jesus rather than to himself since Jesus is the One to whom they will be married. "He must increase, but I must decrease," John says.

This lover-seeking-His-beloved character is precisely what the prophets of the Old Testament expected in the Messiah. Through the prophet Hosea, God expressed the Messianic hope in the form of a beautiful matrimonial overture:

> I will betroth you to Me forever; Yes, I will betroth you to Me In righteousness and justice, In loving kindness and mercy; I will betroth you to Me in faithfulness, And you shall know the Lord. (Hosea 2:19-20)

Jesus came to our world to fulfill this prophecy. Standing before us with the promise of unwavering faithfulness, He offers His proposal of eternal union.

So then, with the bridegroom metaphor in place, John's Gospel proceeds to portray Jesus attracting human hearts to Himself by the alluring beauty of His character. He courts the human heart, step by step, until the climactic revelation of His faithful love is made at the cross. For Jesus, the chosen language for the cross event is the language of attraction. Notice John 12:32: "And I, if I am lifted up from the earth, will draw all peoples to Myself."

His self-sacrificing love is intended to exert a wooing effect upon our hearts. When the courted lady in Solomon's song sings, "I am my beloved's, and His desire is toward me" (Song of Songs 7:10), she is expressing the affectionate response Jesus desires from humanity. The cross is the divine proposal. It is God saying to you and me, "Yes, I have loved you with an everlasting love; therefore with loving kindness I have drawn you" (Jeremiah 31:3).

This is God's heart toward you and me. Jesus came to our world, lived His beautiful life, and then died on the cross for the purpose of revealing His love for us in the hope that we would love Him in return.

And this is the proper context of the Second Coming.

When we come to John 14, we find that Jesus declares to His disciples the promise of His Second Coming by employing the language of matrimonial love that was common to the marriage traditions of their culture. Verses 1-3:

> Let not your heart be troubled; you believe in God, believe also in Me. In My Father's house are many mansions (rooms, in the Greek); if it were not so, I would have told

167

you. I go to prepare a place for you. And if I go and prepare a place for you, I will come again and receive you to Myself; that where I am, there you may be also.

For the ancient near-Eastern culture in which Jesus spoke these words, His meaning was clear. If a man were to propose marriage to a woman and she were to accept the proposal, he would go from her to make preparations for their new life together, departing with the promise of his return. Once all the preparations were made, he would return to escort her to their wedding and to their new home. This is the emotive and affectionate image Jesus chose to employ when making the promise of His Second Coming.

According to Scripture, all those who have said yes to the overtures of Christ's faithful love compose, collectively as one body, His bride. His first advent to our world was for the purpose of setting in motion the courtship phase of His relationship with us. He then departed to prepare a place for us in His Father's house, promising to return one day to receive us to Himself.

Why, then, is Jesus coming again?

Because He is deeply in love with us and wants to be with us forever!

Now then, once it is understood in this light, the promise of His return is so exciting and inviting that we can't help but wonder *when* He will return.

When Will Jesus Come?

Thankfully, Jesus has not left us in the dark on this question. In fact, He quite clearly explained how His followers could know when His coming is near.

In Matthew 24 Jesus engaged in a dialogue with His disciples on this very matter. It was beginning to dawn on them that He would be departing. As we pick up the conversation in Matthew 24:3, He has just told them that Jerusalem and their beloved temple will be completely destroyed:

> Now as He sat on the Mount of Olives, the disciples came to Him privately, saying, "Tell us, when will these things be? And what will be the sign of Your coming, and of the end of the age?"

The disciples can only imagine that the destruction of Jerusalem must mean the end of the world. So Jesus takes this opportunity to delineate a list of signs that will precede His Second Coming and the end of the world. Continuing on with verses 4-14:

And Jesus answered and said to them: "Take heed that no one deceives you. For many will come in My name, saying, 'I am the Christ,' and will deceive many. And you will hear of wars and rumors of wars. See that you are not troubled; for all these things must come to pass, but the end is not yet. For nation will rise against nation, and kingdom against kingdom. And there will be famines, pestilences, and earthquakes in various places. All these are the beginning of sorrows. "Then they will deliver you up to tribulation and kill you, and you will be hated by all nations for My name's sake. And then many will be offended, will betray one another, and will hate one another. Then many false prophets will rise up and deceive many. And because lawlessness will abound, the love of many will grow cold. But he who endures to the end shall be saved. And this gospel of the kingdom will be preached in all the world as a witness to all the nations, and then the end will come.

This prophecy is astoundingly brief and yet comprehensive. Ten signs of the Second Coming are given:

> **Presenter:** *If possible, show this list via PowerPoint or on a board.*

1. False Christ's
2. Wars and rumors of wars
3. Famines
4. Pestilences
5. Earthquakes
6. Persecution
7. False prophets
8. Lawlessness will abound
9. The love of many will grow cold
10. The gospel to all nations

Much of this list definitely matches up with the current state of our world. But we can't help but recognize, too, that most of these things have been going on for hundreds if not thousands of years. How, then, could they constitute unique signs of the Second Coming?

Actually, Jesus anticipated this question and He knew full well that these kinds of things would be going on down through history. So He inserted an ingenious qualification/key to help us pay attention and discern when and in what sense these kinds of things would begin to constitute signs of His Second Coming. This ingenious qualification/key is in verse eight:

All these are the beginning of sorrows.

The English word that is here translated *sorrows* is the Greek word *odin,* which means *birth pains.* So Jesus literally said, *All these things are at the beginning of birth pains.*

> **Presenter:** *Draw the ladies in the audience into a responsive exchange on this point. Something like this: How many of you here tonight have ever given birth?* None of the men, I see, which is good. *Ladies, perhaps you could educate the men here regarding birth pains. What are they like, besides painful? What are the two main characteristics of birth pains?*

Wow, that really brings the matter of end-time signs into perspective. Many of the ladies in the audience know exactly what Jesus is talking about, don't you? Those who have given birth are *painfully* aware that birth pains progress with two main characteristics. As the time for the child to exit the womb approaches, the birth pains increase (1) in frequency and (2) in intensity. So while history has always had wars, famines, pestilences, and earthquakes, Jesus is telling us that as His Second Coming draws near, these types of events will become more and more *frequent* and more and more *intense.* So, then, with this brilliant insight before us we are better able to discern the signs of the times in a sensible manner.

But there is another vital key/qualification as well.

We also notice that all the signs are of a negative nature except one, and that the one positive sign lies within our power to affect. I speak, of course, of the final sign, number ten. Let's read it again, in verse 14:

> And this gospel of the kingdom will be preached in all the world as a witness to all the nations, and then the end will come.

The point Jesus is making is quite clear. All of the negative signs will be monitored and providentially restrained by God in relation to the fulfillment of the one positive sign. In other words, God won't just let the world spin completely out of control with chaos until the good

news of His saving grace is proclaimed to the whole world. He wants every person on the planet to encounter the gospel, the glad tidings, the happy message of His love.
Notice what 2 Peter 3:9 says about the promise of Christ's return and why it hasn't happened yet:

> The Lord is not slack concerning His promise, as some count slackness, but is longsuffering toward us, not willing that any should perish but that all should come to repentance.

This brings us back to the love of God as the reason for the Second Coming, and simultaneously as the reason He hasn't come yet. Jesus is coming because He loves humanity, not because He wants to wreak havoc on our world. He is eager to bring all the evil and suffering of our world to an end as soon as possible. And yet He also longs for the eternal salvation of every person. This is where the final sign comes into play and trumps all the others. God tempers the first nine signs, holding chaotic and evil forces in check in relation to the fulfillment of the tenth sign, which is the gospel proclaimed to every nation. Of course, we can't know precisely when Jesus will come. But we can know, by assessing the condition of our world, that His coming is very soon, contingent upon the one paramount factor of the gospel going to the whole world.

This brings us to our third and final question: how will Jesus come?

How Will Jesus Come?

This may seem like an odd question, but really it's not, because there is much confusion regarding the manner of Christ's Second Coming. Some people have been taught that the Second Coming is merely a mystical and personal event that occurs when Jesus comes into an individual's heart, rather than an anticipated historic event for the world as a whole. Many more have been taught that the Second Coming will be a secret rapture event in which all Christians will suddenly vanish into thin air one day.

But what does Scripture actually teach regarding the manner of Christ's Second Coming?

Acts 1:9-11 brings great clarity to this important issue:

> Now when He had spoken these things, while they watched, He was taken up, and a cloud received Him out of their sight. And while they looked steadfastly toward heaven as He went up, behold, two men stood by them in white apparel, who also said, "Men of Galilee, why do you stand gazing up into heaven? This same Jesus, who was taken up from you into heaven, will so come in like manner as you saw Him go into heaven."

Two points are super-evident in this passage:

1. Jesus was "taken up" into a cloud as the disciples "watched" His departure.
2. Jesus will return to earth in the same "manner" that they saw Him depart.

From this Scripture we can be certain that the Second Coming of Jesus will be a literal, visible event that all human beings will encounter at the same time. Let's look at a few more Scriptures that clarify the manner in which Christ will return to earth.

In the book of Revelation, chapter one, verse seven, the apostle John tells us definitively that the Second Coming will be a universal and visible event:

> Behold, He is coming with clouds, and every eye will see Him.

Jesus Himself described His Second Coming as a glorious and visible event that will be seen in the heavens:

First notice Matthew 16:27:

> For the Son of Man will come in the glory of His Father with His angels, and then He will reward each according to his works.

And Matthew 24:27:

> For as the lightning comes from the east and flashes to the west, so also will the coming of the Son of Man be.

Every eye will see Him!

Attended by His Father and all His holy angels, emitting their collective glory!

Like lightning flashing from the east to the west!

This doesn't sound at all like a mystical event or a secret event. What it sounds like is a cataclysmic historic event that will arrest the attention of the entire world. And that's precisely what it will be.

The apostle Paul expands the picture with additional detail in 1 Thessalonians 4:15-17:

For this we say to you by the word of the Lord, that we who are alive and remain until the coming of the Lord will by no means precede those who are asleep. [16] For the Lord Himself will descend from heaven with a shout, with the voice of an archangel, and with the trumpet of God. And the dead in Christ will rise first. [17] Then we who are alive and remain shall be caught up together with them in the clouds to meet the Lord in the air. And thus we shall always be with the Lord.

We see here, first of all, that the Second Coming will involve the resurrection of all who have ever died "in Christ." Can you imagine what that will be like? We're talking here about millions of deceased men and women coming back to life again. What an amazing event this will be! Secondly, this Scripture tells us that the righteous who are alive during the glorious event will be united with the resurrected righteous to form one massive company who will eagerly meet Jesus in the air.

On the sad and tragic side of Christ's Second Coming, in 2 Thessalonians 2:8 Paul tells us that "the Lord Jesus will overthrow with the breath of his mouth and destroy with the brightness of His coming."

2 Peter 3:10 also sounds this sad note:

> The day of the Lord will come as a thief in the night, in which the heavens will pass away with a great noise, and the elements will melt with fervent heat; both the earth and the works that are in it will be burned up.

So three converging events will occur when Jesus comes:

1. All the wicked who are alive when He returns will be slain.

2. All the righteous of past history will be raised to new life.

3. All those who are alive at His coming will be caught up together with the resurrected righteous to meet the Lord in the air, and "thus shall we ever be with the Lord."

To Be With Us

But now, it's that little word "with" that we want to lastly turn our attention toward—"thus shall we ever be *with* the Lord"—because this word brings us back full circle to *why* Jesus is coming and helps us calibrate our hearts to His passionate longing.

Just before departing from our world, Jesus offered a prayer to the Father that grants us insight to why He came to our world the first time and why He is coming back again. Pay attention to the word *with* in the passage. John 17:24-26:

> "Father, I desire that they also whom You gave Me may be with Me where I am, that they may behold My glory which You have given Me; for You loved Me before the foundation of the world. O righteous Father! The world has not known You, but I have known You; and these have known that You sent Me. And I have declared to them Your name, and will declare it, that the love with which You loved Me may be in them, and I in them."

This is astoundingly simple and beautiful. Jesus describes His ultimate *desire* in terms of wanting you and me to be *with* Him. And why does He want us to be *with* Him? So that we can be brought into the intimate inner circle of love that exists between Him and His Father.

Astounding!

With is a small word that holds huge significance in Scripture. It shows up over and over again. As we discovered in our first message, God is a social being. Said another way, God is all about being *with* others. Consider John 1:1-2:

> In the beginning was the Word, and the Word was with God, and the Word was God. He was in the beginning with God.

Here we see that, "In the beginning. . .God. . .was. . .with God." At first glance, this might seem like a strange thing to say, until we recall that God is portrayed in Scripture as a communitarian kind of being, composed of Father, Son, and Holy Spirit. What this text is telling us is that Jesus, who is fully God, was always *with* the Father, who is also fully God. Later on in the chapter, in verse 18, we read that Jesus "is in the bosom of the Father." The Phillip's Translation says that Jesus "lives in the closest intimacy *with* the Father." There's the word *with* again. God is a *with* kind of being—not an isolationist or a loner, but rather a sociable God who likes to be *with* others.

Matthew 1:23 calls Jesus by a name that communicates God's desire to be with us:

They shall call His name Immanuel, which is translated, "God with us."

174

When the apostle John articulates the grand objective of the gospel, the bottom line is God's desire to have fellowship *with* us. Notice 1 John 1:1-4:

> That which was from the beginning, which we have heard, which we have seen with our eyes, which we have looked upon, and our hands have handled, concerning the Word of life—the life was manifested, and we have seen, and bear witness, and declare to you that eternal life which was with the Father and was manifested to us—that which we have seen and heard we declare to you, that you also may have fellowship with us; and truly our fellowship is with the Father and with His Son Jesus Christ. And these things we write to you that your joy may be full.

Wow, what a testimony!

John says that he *saw* God with his own eyes, *heard* Him speak with his own ears, *touched* Him with his own hands, and had personal fellowship with Him. And then John tells us that this is the hope held out to us all. What a stunning picture of God's coming kingdom! It's all about joyful fellowship with God. This is why Jesus is coming back, my friend. And what a totally amazing thing it will be:

To See Him. As the sky peels open and lights up with glorious brightness, Jesus will draw near in a cloud of angels, closer and closer, until His visible person will take on vivid shape before our eyes. Our hearts will begin to race with excitement. Closer He will descend until we begin to make out His facial features. Finally, we will find ourselves in His immediate presence, eye to eye with the One who is everything to us. And in those eyes we will read nothing but unreserved acceptance.

To Hear Him. What a thrilling thing it will be to hear His voice! That sweet, affirming voice! What will He say? Things like, "Well done, good and faithful servant." And, "I have loved you with an everlasting love." He will speak, and you will become familiar with the audible voice of the One who spoke worlds into existence and had gently whispered forgiveness over your heart so many times throughout life in this rough world.

To Touch Him. And what an experience it will be to actually touch Jesus and be touched by Him! Can you imagine reaching out your hand to literally touch the One who gave His life for you? Or most likely He will reach out to touch you first. His hand on your shoulder, on your cheek, clasping your hand. Your head pressed to His chest with your arms wrapped around Him, and His arms engulfing you. His lips pressed gently to your face to kiss away tears of pain and draw forth tears of joy.

175

Yes, you will see Him.

You will hear him.

You will touch Him.

Jesus is coming again for one reason:

Because He wants to be with you!

Because He is the heavenly Bridegroom eager to receive His bride and be with her forever!

And so it is that the book of Revelation envisions the Second Coming as a glorious wedding to come. Revelation 19:6-8:

> I heard, as it were, the voice of a great multitude, as the sound of many waters and as the sound of mighty thunderings, saying, "Alleluia! For the Lord God Omnipotent reigns! Let us be glad and rejoice and give Him glory, for the marriage of the Lamb has come, and His wife has made herself ready." And to her it was granted to be arrayed in fine linen, clean and bright, for the fine linen is the righteous acts of the saints.

And Revelation 21:1-3:

> Now I saw a new heaven and a new earth, for the first heaven and the first earth had passed away. Also there was no more sea. Then I, John, saw the holy city, New Jerusalem, coming down out of heaven from God, prepared as a bride adorned for her husband. And I heard a loud voice from heaven saying, "Behold, the tabernacle of God is with men, and He will dwell with them, and they shall be His people. God Himself will be with them and be their God.

The bridegroom is coming for His bride! The New Jerusalem, filled with the beloved people of God, redeemed by the precious blood of Jesus, will forever bear the beauty of a bride in the eyes of the One who is our Bridegroom. This is the closing message of the Bible. Jesus is coming again. He's coming for you. He's coming because He loves you and desires that you would be with Him forever.

Is it your desire to be with Him?

Do you long for His soon return?

If so, please respond with your heart to Him as I pray.

PRESENTER, PLEASE SHARE WITH YOUR AUDIENCE THAT THIS IS A SAFE ZONE.
It's a safe place to be themselves. • Everyone has the right to their own opinion.
There are no dumb questions. • All comments are encouraged and respected.

Discussion Questions

1. Have you ever thought of Jesus as "being in love with you"? How does that make you feel? With your group, explore both positive and negative reactions.

2. What have you believed or been taught in the past about Jesus' Second Coming? Have your views changed, and if so, why?

3. What did you think about the "birth pangs" analogy?

4. Do you think it's true that crisis events have been increasing in intensity and number in recent years?

5. Do you believe the coming is near? Why or why not?

6. Whom are you waiting to see again one day?

7. What does it mean for you to "live forever with the Lord"? Are you looking forward to it? If not, what would need to change?

THE MAKER

THE COMMUNICATOR

THE KING

THE SAVIOR

THE SPIRIT

THE GREAT GIVER

THE HEALER

THE SACRIFICE

THE NEW MAN

THE MESSENGER

THE BRIDEGROOM

THE BODY

12. THE BODY

discipleship and the great commission

BIBLE TEXT: Now you are the body of Christ, and members individually. (I Corinthians 12:27)

PRESENTER'S NOTE: On page 187 you will need to insert personal stories about mentoring and being mentored.

Prepare your stories ahead of time.

the **BODY** synopsis

Telling them that it would be to their advantage, Jesus left His followers, seemingly alone, several weeks after His crucifixion and resurrection. Ten days later, their world was turned upside down when the Holy Spirit arrived in power, as promised. He brought with Him gifts for the new church that made it possible for it to operate to this day as the body of Christ on earth, united in amazing diversity. This message examines three basic roles: members, mentors, and missionaries. The first two are active within the church, learning and teaching their individual gifts and how to use them for God's work in the world. The last operates from within the church, reaching outside to seek, save, serve, and sacrifice for the good of others and the glory of God.

The Body

The Sometimes Strange Words of Jesus

Jesus often said things that sounded unusual to His followers. His parables and teachings were not always easily grasped even by those closest to Him. Often the disciples would pull Jesus away privately and ask Him the meaning of some parable or saying which He'd spoken. But of all the seemingly confusing and unusual things that Jesus said, surely none was stranger than this: "Nevertheless I tell you the truth, it is to your advantage that I go away" (John 16:7).

What? How could this possibly be? How, in any sense, could it be to His followers' benefit for Jesus to leave them? At this point in the gospel story, the disciples have no understanding of Jesus' soon-to-come crucifixion, much less His resurrection and ascension. This being the case, Jesus' words must have sounded very strange indeed to the disciples.

But sure enough, just as He had foretold, He was betrayed, crucified, and buried. The disciples were predictably devastated. Though Jesus had repeatedly spoken of His resurrection that would follow, they seem to have been entirely incapable of hearing, much less fully understanding, His words.

And then came Sunday morning. The best Sunday morning the world has ever yet known!

Some of Jesus' women followers had gone to the tomb to finish the preparations they had begun on Friday. When they arrived they were surprised to find... the... tomb...

Empty.

Empty!?

Yes, empty!

Their disappointment-turned-surprise now turned to joy! Their first instinct, upon hearing the words of the angel, "He is not here, but risen!" was to race back to the sorrowing others and tell them—what else?—the GOOD NEWS! The gospel!

Jesus is *alive!* He is *risen!* Just as He had said He would.

In the days following, Jesus revealed Himself to His downcast and confused followers. He spent many days with them, teaching, preaching, and explaining.

Then, in keeping with His custom, He did something, yet again, that they must have found very confusing. And what was that?

He left them, seemingly, alone.

The Birth of the Church

His instructions to them, in anticipation of His departure, were simple enough: stay in Jerusalem and "wait for the Promise of the Father" (Acts 1:4). They obeyed, and ten days later their world was turned upside down. The Holy Spirit, the very "promise of the Father" of which Jesus had spoken, showed up with miraculous power. Luke records this experience in thrilling detail:

> When the Day of Pentecost had fully come, they were all with one accord in one place. And suddenly there came a sound from heaven, as of a rushing mighty wind, and it filled the whole house where they were sitting. Then there appeared to them divided tongues, as of fire, and one sat upon each of them. And they were all filled with the Holy Spirit and began to speak with other tongues, as the Spirit gave them utterance. And there were dwelling in Jerusalem Jews, devout men, from every nation under heaven. And when this sound occurred, the multitude came together, and were confused, because everyone heard them speak in his own language. Then they were all amazed and marveled, saying to one another, "Look, are not all these who speak Galileans? And how is it that we hear, each in our own language in which we were born? Parthians and Medes and Elamites, those dwelling in Mesopotamia, Judea and Cappadocia, Pontus and Asia, Phrygia and Pamphylia, Egypt and the parts of Libya adjoining Cyrene, visitors from Rome, both Jews and proselytes, Cretans and Arabs—we hear them speaking in our own tongues the wonderful works of God." (Acts 2:1-11)

The first gift that the Holy Spirit bestowed on the young church was the ability to speak in languages and dialects that were not their own. This would be exactly the kind of practical gifting they would need if they were going to obey Jesus' startling commission to them:

> Go into all the world and preach the gospel to every creature. He who believes and is baptized will be saved; but he who does not believe will be condemned. And these signs will follow those who believe: In My name they will cast out demons; they will speak with new tongues. (Mark 16:15-17)

And now, on the day of Pentecost, surrounded by people from dozens of countries and areas, Jesus' promise of a "Helper" was beginning to make more sense with each passing second. "Hadn't He said it so clearly," they must've thought, "and here it's happening right before our eyes."

Jesus' once confusing words now rang clear as a bell: "Nevertheless I tell you the truth. It is to your advantage that I go away; for if I do not go away, the Helper will not come to you; but if I depart, I will send Him to you" (John 16:7).

The Helper—the Holy Spirit!—was here! And, what's more, He brought ministry-equipping gifts with Him.

Acts chapter two is, in many ways, the birth of the church. Consider the last few verses of Acts 2:

> And with many other words he testified and exhorted them, saying, "Be saved from this perverse generation." Then those who gladly received his word were baptized; and that day about three thousand souls were added to them. And they continued steadfastly in the apostles' doctrine and fellowship, in the breaking of bread, and in prayers... So continuing daily with one accord in the temple, and breaking bread from house to house, they ate their food with gladness and simplicity of heart, praising God and having favor with all the people. And the Lord added to the church daily those who were being saved. (Acts 2:40-42, 46, 47)

What a day it had been! Peter and the others had preached on that Pentecost day. What had they preached? That Jesus was the long-expected Messiah, and that He had been tragically and torturously killed by some of His own people. But forgiveness was available! After all, hadn't some of Jesus' very last words been, "Father, forgive them, for they do not know what they do" (Luke 23:34)?

So the church was born, and what a birth it was! The seeds that Jesus had planted were now being watered by the Holy Spirit Himself. The disciples must've called to mind the words of Jesus, "Most assuredly, I say to you, unless a grain of wheat falls into the ground and dies, it remains alone; but if it dies, it produces much grain" (John 12:24).

Jesus *was* that grain of wheat that had died.

But His death produced life—much grain!

The Church as the Body of Christ

Probably the most insightful and unusual picture of what the church is called to be is found in Paul's writings. He called it, of all things, "the body of Christ." "Now you are the body of Christ, and members individually" (1 Corinthians 12:27).

> For as the body is one and has many members, but all the members of that one body, being many, are one body, so also is Christ. For by one Spirit we were all baptized into one body—whether Jews or Greeks, whether slaves or free—and have all been made to drink into one Spirit. For in fact the body is not one member but many. If the foot should say, "Because I am not a hand, I am not of the body," is it therefore not of the body? And if the ear should say, "Because I am not an eye, I am not of the body," is it therefore not of the body? If the whole body were an eye, where would be the hearing? If the whole were hearing, where would be the smelling? But now God has set the members, each one of them, in the body just as He pleased. And if they were all one member, where would the body be? But now indeed there are many members, yet one body. (1 Corinthians 12:12-20)

Though the metaphor may seem unusual at first, it is, in fact, perfect. A body, after all, is *one* body, but is made of *many* different kinds of parts. So the idea of the church as the body of Christ on earth expresses, at once, both unity and diversity! Don't miss that! Let me say it again: the body metaphor expresses *both unity and diversity!*

The parts are different and serve their own specialized role, yes, but the role they play furthers the whole, the body *itself.* So both unity and diversity are expressed.

Diversity of roles, but unity of purpose!

Let's listen again to Paul as he develops further still the picture:

> There are diversities of gifts, but the same Spirit. There are differences of ministries, but the same Lord. And there are diversities of activities, but it is the same God who works all in all. But the manifestation of the Spirit is given to each one for the profit of all: for to one is given the word of wisdom through the Spirit, to another the word of knowledge through the same Spirit, to another faith by the same Spirit, to another gifts of healings by the same Spirit, to another the working of miracles, to another prophecy, to another discerning of spirits, to another different kinds of tongues, to another the interpretation of tongues. But one and the same Spirit works all these things, distributing to each one individually as He wills. (1 Corinthians 12:4-11)

Wow! What a grand celebration of variety and of the different gifts, talents, strengths, and interests found in a diverse group of people. After all, isn't it clear, isn't it inescapably obvious? *People are different!*

It stands to reason, then, that God quite obviously values variety. Just look around. People are tall, short, thick, thin, male, female, brown, tan, white, red, black, young, old, and more. Some have curly hair, some straight. Some have big noses, others barely have noses! You get the idea. **(NOTE TO PRESENTER: This is a joke. So laugh!)**

And Paul's point, which is really God's point, of course, is that *everybody is important.*

Since Jesus is in heaven, as we have learned, acting as our High Priest and Advocate in the sanctuary above, He has left two representatives on earth. These representatives are, in a sense, really *one* representative. Their job is to carry forward the work that Jesus began.

Who are these two representatives that are, in a sense, one?

The church and the Holy Spirit.

The Holy Spirit fills the church with His presence, and the church, as it were, gives the Holy Spirit millions of arms, hands, legs, feet, hearts, and eyes!

What a beautiful picture!

Remember those words from the closing verse of Acts 2? "And the Lord added to the church daily those who were being saved" (verse 47). According to this passage, then, when someone comes to faith in Christ and is baptized, they are added to the church.

So let's talk a little about what it means to be "in the church," shall we? We'll consider three areas:

1. Members
2. Mentors
3. Missionaries

Church Members

Being a church member means far more than sitting in a pew on Sabbath morning. It means that you believe and belong. You *believe* the teachings of Scripture, many of which we've covered in this very series. Above all, it means that you *believe* that Jesus Christ is your personal Savior, Priest, King, and Friend. And it also means that, well, you *belong* to a really special group of people who, though different from you and from one another, *believe* the same things!

So members believe and belong.

Members are also *baptized*.

Remember back to the day of Pentecost when Peter and the others were preaching. This is what Luke wrote: "Then those who gladly received his word were baptized; and that day about three thousand souls were added to them" (Acts 2:41). So baptism is a ceremony of entrance into "the body of Christ." Paul actual says this very thing: "For by one Spirit we were all baptized into one body—whether Jews or Greeks, whether slaves or free— and have all been made to drink into one Spirit" (1 Corinthians 12:13). And consider Colossians 1:24 as well, "I now rejoice in my sufferings for you... for the sake of His body, which is the church."

So when someone confesses their personal belief and confidence in the life, death, and resurrection of Jesus by water baptism, then they are baptized into Jesus Christ, into His Body, which is the church!

So we become the hands, feet, ears, and eyes of Jesus Christ on earth. Can there be a higher calling than that? Indeed not! We can love others like Jesus did. We can extend the praying and healing ministry of Jesus. We can extend the teaching and preaching ministry of Jesus. We can extend the social ministry of Jesus. We can extend the discipling ministry of Jesus.

Ah, yes, the ministry of discipleship. Let's turn our attention to that, though with a slightly different word.

Church Mentorship

When someone first joins the body of Christ, they are new, both in belief and in belonging. It may take a little while to get adjusted to this new culture. And it is a culture indeed, complete with its own vocabulary, meetings, ceremonies, social group, and more. But though the church *has* a culture, it is far *more* than a culture. It is a movement, a movement of destiny, divinity, and purpose!

There's so much more to the church than just being a member. Once a new member is acclimated and adjusted, and perhaps even before this, mentorship begins. Mentorship is the same idea as discipleship. Mentorship just means to advise, counsel, teach, and encourage. This is just what Jesus did for His disciples. He taught and trained them and instructed and inspired them. He mentored them!

When a new member comes into the church, they need to be embraced, not baptized and ignored. Or as someone once said: dipped and then dropped! No way! They need encouragement and instruction to deal with their newfound identity in Jesus Christ. Confessing Christ is not always easy, not at all. It can put one at serious odds with his or her family, friends, co-workers, and associates. In some countries and areas, confessing Christ can place someone in real physical danger. This new faith, then, needs to be nurtured, protected, and encouraged.

The church has a responsibility to new members! That responsibility? Mentorship, support, and prayer. Are you a church member? Then you should be mentoring/discipling someone else. Or you should be receiving mentoring/discipling. Or, best of all, you should be doing both!

Consider the words of Paul in 2 Timothy 2:2 in this regard: "And the things that you have heard from me among many witnesses, commit these to faithful men who will be able to teach others also." Did you follow that? Let's break it down. Paul is a mentor to a young pastor named Timothy. He writes to Timothy, encouraging him, among other things, to teach others what Paul has taught him. But there's more; Paul encourages Timothy to teach others who will be able to teach still others. This is mentorship! Just as in a family, the older and more experienced are looking out for the younger and less experienced. So being a member of the body of Christ is about more than mere membership. That's just the start. It also includes growing ourselves under the instruction, encouragement, and help of others, and also helping others to grow under our own instruction, encouragement, and assistance.

> **Presenter:** *This would be a great place to include one or more stories about your own experience in being mentored or in mentoring others. If you, sadly, have not experienced much or any mentorship and guidance, then tell the story of how that has been difficult for you, and how it's made your journey harder than it otherwise needed to be. This is a great opportunity to speak openly, honestly, and yet encouragingly about your own experience in the church. So do it! And remember, be yourself.*

We've looked at membership and mentorship; let's look at the church's mission and missionaries.

Church Mission and Missionaries

If the church is, as we have seen, "the body of Christ" on earth, then we should ask the question: what is its mission and purpose? Fortunately, this is easily answered. We need only ask: What was Jesus Christ's mission and purpose?

The answer to this question is simple and sublime. Jesus Himself said it best in two passages:

> "For the Son of Man has come to seek and to save that which was lost."
> (Luke 19:10)

> "The Son of Man did not come to be served, but to serve, and to give His life a ransom for many." (Matthew 20:28)

There it is: seeking, saving, serving, and sacrificing.

Let's say it together: Seeking. Saving. Serving. Sacrificing.

These are the church's marching orders. More than orders, they are the church's great privilege. This is the church's mission.

Seeking

This is just what it sounds like—being on the look-out for spiritual interests. We are to encourage spiritual interests wherever we find them, and we are to try and create them wherever they are not found. People, all people, are by nature spiritual beings with spiritual interests, but sometimes this can be hidden, either intentionally or unintentionally. The secular world in which many of us find ourselves encourages people to deny or downplay their spiritual interests, inclinations, and investigations. But the longings are often there, sometimes just under the surface and, like miners looking for gold, we need to find and help uncover that interest. This happens through friendships, social connections, at school, work, play, or, really, anywhere. Get out there; meet people; interact; and pray that God will show you how to awaken and discover spiritual interests in people. Go seeking! What we're looking for is more precious than gold!

Saving

The church, of course, does not save anybody. It's Jesus who saves. But it's the church that, remember, is now "the body of Christ." We don't save, but we can *be* the love of Jesus in our family, among our friends, and in our respective communities. We can introduce people to Him, the *only* Savior. The early church understood this and understood it well; listen to Peter in Acts 4:12: "Nor is there salvation in any other, for there is no other name under heaven given among men by which we must be saved." Are you a member of the church? Then you're more than a member, you're a mentor and a missionary! If you're not a member of the church, then, please, by all means accept my sincere appeal right now to become one by trusting in Him alone who can save you, Jesus Christ.

> **Presenter:** *Make a "mini" appeal right here. Perhaps invite people who are considering putting their faith in Jesus Christ to raise their hands.*

HELPFUL TIPS

Serving

If Jesus was anything, He was a Servant! Go read John 13 and see how He serves His disciples by washing their dirty, grimy feet. As a servant, He invites us, His followers, to serve: "If I then, your Lord and Teacher, have washed your feet, you also ought to wash one another's feet. For I have given you an example, that you should do as I have done to you" (John 13:14, 15). Foot washing was, in the time of Jesus, a menial and servile task that just, well, had to be done. But no one *wanted* to wash the dusty, dirty, and smelly feet of others. But Jesus did. He was Himself God, but foot washing was not beneath Him. He was the truest kind of leader; He was a *servant* leader. He led by example and influence, not by position and power. If He was a servant, then the church is offered the privilege of service as well. To feed the hungry, give water to the thirsty, clothe the naked, shelter the homeless, parent the orphan, encourage the widow, and so, so much more. Service is the business of the church because it was the business of Jesus. *Any true church is in some way seeking to serve and better its community.*

Sacrificing

Jesus, of course, literally sacrificed Himself. But even before this, He sacrificed His time, talents, resources, and energies. We are called to do the same—to live lives of sacrificial sincerity, denying ourselves some things we might love to have in order to bless and benefit others. It is in giving that we truly receive. Life comes when we give, not when we seek to keep and gain as much as we can. "For what will it profit a man if he gains the whole world, and loses his own soul" (Mark 8:36)? "Take heed and beware of greed, for one's life does not consist in the abundance of the things he possesses" (Luke 12:15).

True happiness is found in sacrificially serving others. Sure, it's not always easy, but it's always *worth it in the end.* "He who finds his life will lose it, and he who loses his life for My sake will find it" (Matthew 10:39). Maybe you can volunteer at a local shelter? Or perhaps you can be a big brother or sister to someone who needs one? Perhaps you have some clothes that you can donate? Or some time? Or money? Perhaps God is calling you to give or to pray in a sacrificial way for some person, family, situation, or ministry? Perhaps God is calling you to start your own ministry of service. There are millions of ways you can sacrifice some of your abundance for those who have less; *because there are always those with less.*

So, seeking, saving, serving, and sacrificing.

This is what it means to be a missionary for God's church, which is Christ's own body on earth. God is calling you to be a member, a mentor, and a missionary. Will you accept that call and pray for the filling and equipping of the Holy Spirit?

We've come, at last, to the final part of this first series, and what a journey it has been! We've learned point by point, step by step about *The One*, Jesus Christ. And do you know what? We've learned that He *really is The One!* He is Maker, King, Savior, Healer, Life, Bridegroom and much more besides. We've seen so many beautiful and diverse pictures of Him and, the truth be told, we're only just getting started! The journey has just begun!

Jesus Christ is *The One,* but here's an amazing turn of events: He believes that *you* are *the one*.

Yes, you!

He is calling you to believe in Him, to trust Him, and to be His special child. He wants you as a member of His body and as an eternal companion and friend. He is calling you. Won't you respond to Him?

The One is calling you to Himself. Come to Him. Trust Him. Believe Him. Live for Him. Worship Him. Serve Him. Bring others to Him.

For He is worthy of your loyalty and love. He is the one your heart desires, for He made your heart *to* desire Him! Hear His word, just now, and believe it: "If the Son makes you free, you shall be free indeed" (John 8:36). "The thief does not come except to steal, and to kill, and to destroy. I have come that they may have life, and that they may have it more abundantly" (John 10:10). "Come to Me, all you who labor and are heavy laden, and I will give you rest" (Matthew 11:28).

Truly, He is *The One!*

PRESENTER, PLEASE SHARE WITH YOUR AUDIENCE THAT THIS IS A SAFE ZONE.
It's a safe place to be themselves. • Everyone has the right to their own opinion.
There are no dumb questions. • All comments are encouraged and respected.

Discussion Questions

1. Try to imagine that you are one of Jesus' disciples when He says He's leaving, "but don't worry, you'll be glad in the end." How do you think you would have felt?

2. Now imagine that He is dead and buried. Now how would you feel?

3. Next, imagine that you are in the upper room on the day of Pentecost. Now how do you feel?! How long do you think it would take as you grew into the full understanding of what Jesus meant when He said His leaving would be to our advantage?

4. Discuss the concept of the church as body of Christ. Can you think of some analogies? Some who are like feet, or hands, or ears?

5. Where do you fit in the member, mentor, and missionary categories? Depending on answers within your group, discuss:

   a. What it means to be a member; is there more help you feel you need, either to become a member or as a member now?

   b. What it means to be a mentor; is there more help you feel you need, either to become a mentor or as a mentor now?

   c. What it means to be a missionary; is there more help you feel you need,